D0364566

Fifty Years With Mountbatten

Fifty Years With Mountbatten

A PERSONAL MEMOIR
by his
Valet and Butler

CHARLES SMITH

SIDGWICK & JACKSON
LONDON

First Published in Great Britain in 1980
by Sidgwick and Jackson Limited

Edited by Don Short.

ISBN 0 283 98677 8

Printed in Great Britain by
The Garden City Press Limited
Pixmore Avenue, Letchworth, Hertfordshire SG6 1JS
for Sidgwick and Jackson Limited
1 Tavistock Chambers, Bloomsbury Way
London WC1A 2SG

Contents

List of Illustrations   5

Introduction   9

1   Early Days   15
2   Travelling Footman to Lady Mountbatten   21
3   On the Bus with Prince Philip   33
4   Putting a Zip In It!   45
5   Abdication   51
6   War   58
7   To India with the Viceroy   71
8   A Royal Marriage   83
9   Domestic Duties   90
10   A Brandy for Sir Winston!   104
11   The Death of Lady Louis   115
12   Charles – Butler or Prince?   134
13   The Loneliness of Lord Louis   150
14   The Last Farewell   158

Epilogue   171

Index   173

List of Illustrations

All the illustrations were supplied by the author from his private collection or have been taken from his cine films.

PHOTOGRAPHS

Charles Smith   *frontispiece*
  (photo by Terry Fincher, Photographers International)

                                                                 facing page
My parents, Edith and John   16
Aged seventeen, schoolroom footman with Lord and Lady
Derby   16
Adsdean   17
With Sabi, the Mountbattens' pet lion   17
Bozo the bush baby   32
Rastas the honey bear   32
Christmas card from Lord and Lady Louis, 1941   33

Lady Patricia's wedding (P.A.-Reuter)   48
On board the royal yacht *Victoria and Albert*   49
As an R.A.F. sergeant   49
Viceroy and Vicereine of India   64
Gandhi and Lord Louis taking tea   65
Lord Louis' York MW102   65

facing page

Princess Elizabeth and Prince Philip in Romsey   80
Coronation photograph, 1953 (photo by Baron)   80
Lee Lodge, Broadlands   81
The lounge of our stable yard cottage   81
The stables at Broadlands (photo by the author)   96
Putting the finishing touches to Lord Louis' uniform   96
Lady Pamela's wedding (Associated Press)   97

Between pages 112 and 113
Lord Louis playing with Juno's puppies (photo by the author)
Princess Margarita of Sweden, Lord Louis and the King of Sweden
     (photo by the author)
Charlie and Oona Chaplin, Lord Louis, and Lord and Lady
     Brabourne in the grounds of Broadlands (photo by the author)
Lord Louis and Charlie Chaplin (photo by the author)
Lord Louis and the Queen of Thailand (photo by the author)
The Duchess of Windsor and Lord Louis (photo by the author)
The Duke of Windsor planting a sapling (photo by the author)
The Duke of Windsor about to hand me a tip (photo by the author)

facing page

Lord Louis with his labrador Pancho (photo by the author)   128
With Violet before attending a Garden Party at Buckingham
     Palace   128
With some of the gifts given to Violet and myself over the
     years during our service with Lord and Lady Louis
(photo by Terry Fincher, Photographers International)   129

page

Lord Mountbatten's inscription to Charles Smith on the title
     page of *Louis & Victoria: The First Mountbattens* by Richard
     Hough   109
Christmas greeting from H.R.H. Prince Charles   142
Invitation from H.M. the Queen to her silver wedding Thanks-
     giving Service in Westminster Abbey, 20 November 1972   143
Lord Mountbatten's inscription to Charles Smith on the half-
     title page of *The Life and Times of Lord Mountbatten* by John
     Terraine   155

LETTERS

page

From Lord Mountbatten, South-East Asia Command Headquarters, 21 August 1945   63

—— Broadlands, 29 October 1946   74

—— Ministry of Defence, 31 October 1962   95

—— Ministry of Defence, 3 July 1961   96

—— Broadlands, 15 February 1968   100

—— Wilton Crescent, London, 8 February 1951   102

—— Commander-in-Chief, Mediterranean, 28 July 1954   107

—— Ministry of Defence, 16 July 1959   120

—— cable from London, 23 February 1960   124

—— Broadlands, 25 February 1960   126

—— Ministry of Defence, 8 July 1960   127

—— Ministry of Defence, 22 April 1961   128

—— Christmas, 1960   130

—— Classiebawn Castle, Co. Sligo, 4 June 1972   138

—— Broadlands, 9 January 1970   146

—— Ministry of Defence, 14 June 1962   148

—— New York, 19 March 1968   151

—— Broadlands, 24 June 1970   156

—— Broadlands, 7 March 1973   159

From H.R.H. Prince Charles, H.M.S. *Minerva*, Turks and Caicos Islands, 19 March 1973   160

From Lord Mountbatten, postcard from Kandy, 14 February 1976   166

Introduction

Our rows were sometimes spectacular, but we savoured every turbulent minute of them. They were splendid, tempestuous affairs with no holds barred, our faces often turning crimson under each other's verbal lashings. No other Royal servant in the land held licence to challenge Lord Mountbatten's word. That was one special privilege he granted me, his valet and butler for nearly fifty years.

My right to differ was the foundation stone of our relationship. It formed a bond that no one could break, a unique bond between master and servant that members of Royalty, as well as family and friends, distantly admired.

Lord Louis trusted me, he knew I would never let him down and would never presume to question his authority in public, whatever contentions we cared to air in private.

One particular row I remember. It was in 1977 when Thames Television had secretly made His Lordship the unsuspecting subject for *This Is Your Life*. I dared to question his total innocence of the plot that had led him into their studio lair.

'Someone must have tipped you off, surely m'Lord?' I suggested to Lord Louis.

His Lordship was indignant.

'Charles, don't be so damned stupid,' he retorted, 'I didn't know anything about it. They got me into the studio on some plausible pretext and I fell for it – hook, line and sinker.'

'Rubbish,' I countered dismissively, 'you must have known . . .'

'Charles,' growled His Lordship, 'I'm telling you the truth.'

'They pulled the cotton wool over *your* eyes, m'Lord? I can't believe it. It must have been fixed!'

Lord Louis' fury broke.

'How dare you suggest such a thing,' he thundered. 'One more word of that kind and I'll sue you for slander.'

'Wait a minute, m'Lord,' I said, 'I've been with you for nearly fifty years and not once have you ever stepped outside the door without first knowing the lay of the ground.'

Lord Louis planned every move, reviewed every engagement, with the subtle care of a Grand Master of chess.

'That's so,' agreed His Lordship, 'but this time, Charles, I'm afraid I was taken in.'

'Then, m'Lord, it must certainly have been an elaborate conspiracy,' I said, quietening down.

'It was Charles. It was,' sighed Lord Louis, relieved to think that I was seeing reason.

Indeed, a conspiracy had been carefully laid under the cover of a celebration for his daughter Lady Pamela's birthday.

I realized I was wrong and made my apologies before Lord Louis could issue his writ for slander! I suppose that I was inwardly angry that anyone could have duped His Lordship in the way that they did. It was beyond my comprehension.

Two years later another conspiracy, of a very different and sinister nature, was hatched by the I.R.A., whose cowardly act of treachery did indeed make my master an innocent victim. One for which he was to pay with his life and which brought heartache to the world.

27 August 1979 began just like another day for me. I had been recruited from retirement to act as an official guide in Lord Louis' stately home of Broadlands in Romsey. It had been opened to the public by His Royal Highness Prince Charles in the early summer and since then 198,000 visitors had flocked to see it. At about 1.00 p.m. on the 27th I was on duty in the regal, chintz-layered Portico Room, the most historically romantic room in the house.

'The Portico Room,' I was describing to a group of inquisitive American visitors, 'is probably the most famous room at Broadlands as it is used by Her Majesty Queen Elizabeth and Prince Philip on all their visits and it was here that they spent their honeymoon in 1947, as indeed Lord and Lady Mountbatten did in 1922 . . .'

Before I could continue I felt a tap on my shoulder and Lynette Adams, the guide organizer, whispered to me that news was coming in of an explosion that had occurred in Ireland involving Lord Louis and one of his twin grandchildren, Nicholas, who was reported missing.

'That's all we know,' she said, 'but I thought I should warn you in case any of the visitors question you. They might have heard something on the radio.'

I felt a cold shiver run down my spine.

Before Lord Louis left for Ireland he could have easily asked for extra security, but he did not see himself as a target.

'The I.R.A. are not looking for an old man like me,' he reasoned. 'Besides, I go to Ireland every summer, as you know, Charles. I have never had a moment's trouble. Why should I now?'

It was true. He thought of Classiebawn Castle, his summer home on the breathtaking coastline of County Sligo, as a haven of peace and beauty, not a harbour for murder.

At two o'clock I was relieved of my duty. Descending the staircase to Broadlands' administrative offices I knew by the expressions on the faces that gazed in my direction that the worst had happened.

'Charles,' said one of the staff, barely managing to find his words, 'the news is terrible. The I.R.A. have blown up Lord Louis' boat *Shadow V.* They were all aboard, just going out to sea. Lord Louis is dead and Nicholas too. Lord Brabourne's mother is badly hurt and she is not expected to live . . .'

It was impossible to grasp all that I was hearing. Tears streamed down my cheeks as someone drove me home. The gates of Broadlands were closed.

Lord Louis dead? I would have gladly laid down my own life to spare his, the man in whose shadow I had constantly lived, day in, day out, year after year, sharing his fortunes, his triumphs and tears, his adventures and agonies.

I had been with him through eventful, historic days in many parts of the world: in Singapore as Supreme Allied Commander, where I had seen him accept the surrender of the Japanese; in Delhi, when he was proclaimed Viceroy of India to restore peace and supervise the granting of independence to the riot-stricken sub-continent; in Malta where he was Commander-in-Chief, Mediterranean; and elsewhere.

In travelling through history with Lord Louis for almost half a century, I had witnessed first hand his immense courage and bravery. I had seen, too, a leader whose compassion was manifest for man's plight across the face of the earth. He was a great man and I shall treasure the years I was in service with him.

Lord Louis could not have envisaged the ghastly way in which he was to die, but he was well prepared for death. He had made his will and arranged the most exacting details of his funeral many years before. Even the six scarlet cushions that were to bear his crowns and crests in the cortège had been made at that time and photographed by the Imperial War Museum.

'I don't want to be a bloody nuisance to anybody when I go, Charles,' he explained. 'In this way, everything is done and it's going to save a lot of people a considerable amount of time and trouble.'

It was typical of the way Lord Louis ran his life. Everything had to be properly organized. Efficiency and perfection were two of his main priorities. He could not tolerate slip-ups and he wasn't prepared to accept any excuses — even at his own funeral. When the B.B.C. were preparing his television obituary, he was tickled pink and could not resist their invitation to contribute personally!

I must confess I was a little staggered when His Lordship gave me a bronze plaque, etched with a portrait of himself. 'When I die, Charles, this has got to go into Romsey Abbey.'

His Lordship was then a mere seventy-two and a pillar of strength!

'Why all the gloom, m'Lord?' I asked him.

'Charles,' he replied, 'you've got to be prepared.'

His Lordship was serious about it. A day or two later we went in search of a suitable resting place for him, although I was naive enough to believe we were only going for a morning drive on the estate in my mini. His Lordship hadn't given me an inkling as to his real motives as we set out over Broadlands' 6,600 acres, driving past the home produce farm, the new cow sheds and taking the road out through the forests. But then His Lordship said, 'Would you mind taking me on up to the cemetery on the Botley Road?'

'Of course, m'Lord,' I said, 'but what are you going up there for? You're not surely thinking of copping out yet?'

'No,' smiled His Lordship, 'but I want to make sure that they've got some space left for me when I do!'

We climbed out of the mini and walked round the cemetery on top of the hill where his parents-in-law, Lord and Lady Mount Temple, were laid to rest in a family tomb.

Lord Louis slapped his shoulders against the biting cold. A strong icy wind was blowing. He turned up the collar of his hacking jacket and shuddered, stepping back into the car.

'I don't think I would like it up here. It's a bit too blowy for the old bones, Charles,' he mused.

We drove on to Romsey Abbey, but scanning the complexity of headstones and tombs Lord Louis shook his head.

'It's too damn crowded. They'll never fit me in,' he exclaimed, 'I don't know where they will bury me when I go.'

I don't think it occurred to him at that moment that he might have a tomb inside the Abbey, where he is now finally laid to rest.

There was no desire on his part to be buried at sea as Lady Louis had been on her death in 1960. Throughout their lives together His Lordship had always admired his wife's independent spirit – 'That's Edwina again, doing her own thing.' I suspected that this is what he thought when Her Ladyship decided to be buried at sea.

'But that's not for me, Charles; and what's more, I don't want to be cremated either!' he declared.

Lord Louis said that when he died he wanted people to be jolly and not morbid. That was too much to obey, for any of us, but I know that His Lordship would have approved that his word was kept in every other sense. The funeral was as he wanted it to be.

In twelve grey cardboard boxes safely stowed at Broadlands in a linen room that was no bigger than an attic, Lord Louis had gathered a legacy for his grandchildren and nephews. The legacy was, in effect, his life – mementoes and souvenirs that he had collected over the years. Like a man emptying out his pockets, Lord Louis would reguarly add an assortment of diaries, documents, pens and books, even copies of his public speeches, crests, medals, tokens and relics of his ventures in Burma, Malta, India, and the Far East.

'When I go, Charles,' said Lord Louis, 'the children will be able to open these boxes and learn something more about my life than the historians will be able to tell them.'

Every object placed in the boxes held a specific meaning and message.

Lord Louis delegated me to install the boxes originally and I assisted Mrs Mollie Travis, the archivist, in preserving them. Each one bore the initials of his grandchildren: Norton, Michael-John, Joanna, Amanda, Philip, Nicholas, Timothy, Edwina, Ashley, and India; and of his great-nephews George and Ivar.

Tragically, Nicholas was to die with his grandfather in Ireland, but the nine surviving grandchildren and his two great-nephews will know much today about their famous ancestor in a light that is personal to each one of them.

CHARLES SMITH
Romsey, 1980

1
Early Days

My service with the Mountbattens began in 1930, but before that I was hall boy at the age of fourteen to the Duke and Duchess of Portland, and then footman with Lord and Lady Derby.

I left school when I was twelve, determined to make some mark in the world, though in the depths of rural England only the legends of Robin Hood and his exploits existed to spur me on. Sherwood Forest was my childhood playground, having been raised in the fringing Nottinghamshire villages of Harworth, Hesley and Whitwell.

I was born in Harworth on 7 March 1908, but my parents moved soon after and my first recollections are of Hesley where I attended the village school along with ten or twelve other pupils.

My father, John Smith, was a gardener to Squire Whittaker, master of Hesley Hall, an imposing country house with its own private passage to the village church. His wages were poor, but with the support of my hard-working mother we were never likely to starve. The rambling garden surrounding our tied cottage on the estate produced a yearly profusion of fruit and vegetables and we reared pigs, chickens, ducks, and rabbits, whose fold would vary according to our culinary needs. Aware as a boy of the need to earn money, I chopped schoolmistress Miss Ridgewall's firewood for a penny a week.

I was only six years old when the First World War broke out and it really had no meaning for me until the day my father, who had enlisted with the Sherwood Rangers cavalry, was posted overseas to Salonica. My father's experience on the estate with horses had led to his acceptance in the Rangers and he was to serve as an officer's batman with two horses in his charge.

My poor mother was heartbroken when my father left for the war. I was then the eldest of five; the youngest, twins Dorothy and Jack, were only three months old, and the responsibility weighed heavily upon her.

When the Germans began their Zeppelin raids over England the giant craft would frequently pass overhead, but they retained their bombs for more vital targets than Sherwood Forest. On our way home from school we would stand and watch them through the trees and I would think of my father, not really knowing what part he played in the war. Often I would return from school, or from church where I was a choir boy, and find my mother quietly weeping, wondering whether we would see my father ever again. But his letters home would always cheer her and give her fresh hope.

When the school holidays came round I would go out into the fields with my mother to pick potatoes and peas and stack corn. We only earned a few shillings but it meant a great deal to the household budget.

Saturdays were very special. For one penny we could ride on the stagecoach into Doncaster to go shopping. It was probably one of the last horse-drawn stagecoaches still in service in England, for the age of the motor car had already dawned, although it was still a rare sight on the road.

My father's safe homecoming at the end of the war was a day of rejoicing and he hugged us all endlessly. In our village, as in all parts of the country, 'Welcome Home' streamers and rows of flags crossed the cobbled streets to greet our victorious soldiers, sailors and airmen.

My father was no worse off for the war. He was still the powerful, thick-set man whose strength and weathered hands had come from his labours on the estate where he was to resume his employment as a gardener.

Above: My parents, Edith and John

Right: Aged seventeen, schoolroom footman with Lord and Lady Derby, in the grounds of their house at Coworth Park, near Virginia Water

Adsdean, the lovely country mansion near Chichester that Lord and Lady Louis rented before Lady Louis inherited Broadlands in 1939

At Adsdean with Sabi, the Mountbattens' pet lion that Lady Louis brought back with her from Africa

Fifteen months later, deciding there was no real future for him working on the estate, we moved to the neighbouring hamlet of Whitwell where my father opened a fish and chip shop in the village. Fresh fish supplies would come from Grimsby and these, along with bags of potatoes, would be loaded on to a donkey-drawn cart for the mile-long journey from our house to the shop. I helped my father in the shop, earning three pence a week. I was twelve years old. My school life had come to an abrupt end in Whitwell after only four days. One hiding from the school bully was enough!

My parents were devoted to one another and the family grew. From being the eldest of five, I was eventually to find myself the senior of seven, but by then I was already working.

When I was fourteen I decided to work in a local coal mine. My father raised no objections as I would be able to make a more substantial contribution to the family budget, taking home £2 a week in wages. My first day down the pit was a disappointment – I didn't so much as get my face dirty! Feeling ashamed, I deliberately smudged coal dust on my face to look the part, and only then did I proceed home.

For nearly a year everything went well, but the older miners warned me to watch my health and I came to wish that I had listened more to their advice. Conditions in the pit were poor and there was constant dampness to combat. I developed a series of illnesses – rheumatic fever, scarlet fever and Bright's disease. I had already been operated on at Worksop Hospital for acute appendicitis. My health deteriorated dangerously and at one point I weighed only 4 stone 5 lb and I was not strong enough to walk. My parents summoned a priest who adminstered the last rites; but their prayers for a miracle were rewarded and I began to pull through.

I was sent to an uncle's farm to recuperate, and when my health was restored I made the decision that was to change my life.

Four miles away, commanding the horizon and always the focal point of my eyes, was the seventeeth-century grey-stoned Welbeck Abbey, the home of the Duke and Duchess of Portland. It held considerable fascination for me, and one morning I put on my jacket and breeches – hand-me-downs from the village Squire's son – and cycled to the Abbey. It was approached by a tunnel, one of a labyrinth of passages which remain even today a curious architectural feature of the Abbey. Emerging at the other end of the tunnel I came into a long, straight drive which cut through the finely manicured gardens. Half-way up the drive I nearly lost my nerve, but I pressed my pedals forward and arriving at the massive front door I rang the bell.

A liveried footman answered my call and viewed me with suspicion, especially when he saw my bicycle propped conspicuously against a pillar.

'I am looking for work,' I said meekly.

The footman heaved a sigh. 'Then don't stand there, boy. Get round to the back of the house and find the tradesmen's entrance. This door is only used by the Duke and Duchess and their guests.'

A reassuring glimmer appeared in his eye as he closed the door on me and by the time I got to the rear he had alerted the steward of the house whose task it was to employ the servants. The fact that I was offered the job of hall boy, at £25 a year, was attributed to my sheer nerve in daring to descend on the front door.

As hall boy I had very little contact with the Duke and Duchess; I attended to the whims and needs of the fifty senior servants. In time, however, I qualified by arduous duty for promotion to stewards' room footman, the yearly increment for which was £10. There were also peripheral benefits, including two free suits of clothing a year, special allowances for laundry and beer, the provision of meals, and a comfortable room of my own in the house.

Welbeck Abbey was a magnificent estate with three lakes and a sweeping parkland embracing golf course, tennis courts, bowling greens, cricket and football pitches, as well as sports pavilions. It was here that I learned to play golf, a game in which I was to excel and to become a low handicap player. When I was seventeen I had the opportunity of turning professional by becoming an assistant to the top pro at one of Nottinghamshire's main courses. Alas, a fight at Welbeck Abbey left me with a disjointed arm when I fell to the floor grappling with one of the grooms.

The Duchess of Portland, who was particularly kind, sent me for physiotherapy treatment in London and for three months I had to exercise my injured arm by carrying a heavy bucket of sand in my hand in order to straighten my muscles. Today my right arm is one inch longer than my left. The physician was sceptical about my chances of ever playing golf again, but fortunately I was not entirely forced out of the game and I was able to play on a competitive, if amateur, level.

The Duchess gave help to more needy cases than my own. She worked tirelessly for charity. Invalids would be specially invited to the Abbey and I would assist their wheelchair tours of the estate. The Duchess would also arrange accommodation for injured miners and their families, while in the grounds she built a special paddock and stables to provide shelter for retired and unwanted pit ponies.

I was sorry to leave Welbeck, but after three years I knew it was time to move on, and I took a position as schoolroom footman with Lord and Lady Derby whose home was at Knowsley Hall, near Liverpool. My responsibility was to look after the couple's two grandchildren who had been orphaned by the loss of their father during the war and whose mother, Lady Victoria, had died in a hunting accident.

The Derbys were very much part of England's élite, especially among the racing fraternity. Lord Derby, father-figure of horse racing, would spend his days at Epsom, Ascot, Newmarket, and other similar venues. Racing was infectious within the family; even the grandchildren would have a regular sixpenny flutter which I would place for them!

Every year, after the Epsom Derby – the famous race named after His Lordship's family – a lavish ball would be held in London by my employers. The 1927 celebrations brought a distinguished guest of honour: Charles Lindbergh, the American pilot who had just flown non-stop across the Atlantic in his monoplane.

I was seconded to assist in the resplendent ballroom of Derby House and attired in full footman's livery: a gold and silver embroidered red tail cut-away coat; a stiff-fronted wing-collared shirt and white bow tie; blue velvet knickerbockers; pink silk stockings; and silver-buckled black pumps. My hair was waved and powdered white. From head to tail I was the immaculate footman.

I stayed with Lord and Lady Derby until the early part of 1930 when Mr Brown, their steward, heard on the grapevine that a travelling footman was being sought at Brook House in Park Lane, London.

'Who lives there?' I enquired.

'Why, Lord and Lady Mountbatten,' he replied. 'Why not go for it, Charles? You would be right for it. I know the steward there. I'll give him a ring for you . . .'

2

Travelling Footman to Lady Mountbatten

In Park Lane the soft, early morning sunlight filtered through the trees, which were proudly unfurling their new season's foliage. It was the kind of morning to instil fresh dreams. They were badly needed at that time, for Britain, with nearly 1,500,000 unemployed, was struggling to shake itself free from the Depression.

My own future, at least, looked assured that day of 15 April 1930, although I could have hardly guessed then, as I knocked on the door of elegant Brook House, that I was taking the first step in what was to be a life-long association with the Mountbatten family.

I had put on my best grey suit for the occasion, anxious to create the right impression, and in my hand I carried a small brown suitcase containing my worldly possessions, which were scant: another suit, some casual clothes, and one or two pictures of my family.

I straightened my shoulders as I heard footsteps from inside the hall. Slowly, the big black door, with its brass letter box and handle plates polished brightly, opened. Mr Spencer, the butler who had interviewed me only a few days earlier, was now greeting me.

'Good morning, Charles,' he said warmly, 'welcome to Brook

House. You're in good time. I will take you down to your room and then you must come with me to see Lord and Lady Louis. They like to meet all the new staff.'

As I stepped into the house, I had to shorten my paces to avoid sliding on the marble floors. I was led down to the basement and along a narrow corridor where Mr Spencer threw open a door on the left.

'This will be your room, Charles,' he said, beckoning me forward. 'I hope you will find it comfortable enough. What I suggest you do is unpack your things and I will come to collect you in twenty minutes or so.'

Mr Spencer left me in the small room to gather my thoughts. I looked round at my new home. There was one lattice window overlooking a yard, no bigger than a postage stamp, but it provided sufficient light in the room to see that it was very tastefully decorated and furnished. Carpets were laid on the floor, there were nice curtains, the bed was well sprung and I had a sideboard, writing desk and armchair. There was a toilet and bathroom adjoining. I could not have wished for more. My starting wage was £65 a year.

My knowledge of Lord and Lady Mountbatten was limited. Since their marriage in 1922, they had rarely been out of the newspapers and of course I was well aware of their Royal connections.

Lord Louis was the great-grandson of Queen Victoria, and his aunt was the Tsarina of Russia. His mother, Princess Victoria of Hesse, took charge of his early education and he did not go to school until he was ten (to think I was leaving my village school at the age of twelve!). Determined to follow his father, the First Sea Lord, into the Navy, he enrolled in the Royal Naval College at Osborne. Now, at thirty years of age, he was a Senior Instructor in Wireless Telegraphy at the Signals School at Portsmouth.

Lady Mountbatten, who was Edwina Ashley before her marriage, was a socialite beauty of great intellect and wealth whose grandfather was the millionaire financier Sir Ernest Cassel, a confidante of King Edward VII. The Earl of Shaftesbury and the former premier Lord Palmerston were among her forebears. She was a year and a half younger than her husband.

Their image was formidable and I must confess that as Mr

Spencer conducted me to meet them that morning I was more than a little nervous. My anxieties were quickly allayed, however, for my welcome was a very friendly one. Both Lord and Lady Louis had a wonderful facility for putting people at their ease. Lady Louis was in the drawing room arranging some flowers in a vase. She turned and smiled when Mr Spencer marched me in.

'You must be Charles,' she said sweetly. 'It's very nice of you to come and be my footman. I do hope it won't be too much for you.'

Her Ladyship was wearing a blue costume and she wore a pearl necklace. She gave me the impression of being a very homely woman, which is perhaps a rare quality in someone quite so beautiful. Beauty can often be so cold.

I was hurried on through to meet Lord Louis, who was to be found in his panelled study, poring over some papers on his desk. He was in Naval uniform and when I entered the room with Mr Spencer he stood up to greet me. He shook my hand firmly and said,'I hope you will be happy with us, Charles. Have you seen your room yet?'

I nodded, 'Yes, my Lord. Thank you. It is very comfortable.'

'I am pleased to hear it, Charles. And you know what your duties entail?'

'Yes, m'Lord. I am ready to start,' I said.

Mr Spencer caught my eye and we withdrew, leaving Lord Louis to get back to his paperwork.

My immediate feelings were that the atmosphere at Lord and Lady Louis' home would not be quite so formal as I had experienced in service with Lord Derby. At Lord Derby's, and in those earlier years at Welbeck Abbey too, I had always been called 'Smith' and I was surprised when both Lord and Lady Louis, independently of one another, addressed me as 'Charles'. There was also less formality in my duties. The actual livery of the staff, however, was similar. I wore a black tail coat with black buttons and changed into blue livery in the evening, the jacket having a red collar with silver braid, which also edged my red waistcoat. Only the trousers were plain.

My arrival at Brook House almost coincided with a very special event in the Mountbatten household. Four days after joining the staff Lord and Lady Louis' second infant Miss Pamela celebrated her first birthday. There was a party, to which the domestic staff were on hand to give cheer. Miss Pamela, gurgling with pleasure in her high chair, was clearly aware of what was happening around her. When it came to blowing out the candle on her iced birthday cake she got plenty of instruction from her five-year-old sister Miss Patricia.

Only the previous day Miss Pamela had been my first 'visitor' when I was delegated to keep watch for callers at the front door. She had returned in her pram from an afternoon outing in the park escorted by her nanny. Nanny Woodard, then in fragile years, had some difficulty navigating the pram over the doorstep. I assisted her with it and carried it on through to Miss Pamela's nursery.

Indeed, my first duties in the household generally necessitated waiting on the front door and attending to callers, but as the days passed other tasks were given me. My assistance was required in setting the luncheon and dinner tables, preparing the cocktails and wines, and polishing silver, which was always regarded among the pantry staff as something of a chore, but one they would ultimately regard with pride when the cutlery was gleaming.

My duties as Lady Louis' travelling footman were, of course, quite different when the household was in transit. My priority then was to ensure that Lady Louis travelled comfortably and without concern for the arrangements. I would book and collect her travel tickets, carry her luggage, and on long-distance journeys to the Far East when she was not accompanied by her maid I would find myself pressing Her Ladyship's clothes and washing her 'smalls'. I would set aside Her Ladyship's laundry when she wasn't there and when the garments were washed and properly dried I would return them to her wardrobe. I felt no embarrassment, although I confess to receiving the oddest of stares from hotel chambermaids who must have wondered why I had a frilly line of underwear drying over the bath in my bedroom!

Her Ladyship was fastidious about her clothes; she used to go to Paris in search of new fashions and I was frequently sent over on the Channel ferry to pick up packages and parcels containing fresh orders of her favourite perfumes and cosmetics, or to collect some new shoes that she might have requested. She had very small feet –

she only took a size 3½ shoe. Her shoes were made especially for her by a well established Parisian house.

Lord Louis was equally meticulous, he always cut a fine figure in blazer and flannels, but in those days he was rarely out of Naval uniform. In time I persuaded him to become more fashion conscious and actually shook him out of his conservative ideas to try a new tailor!

Lord and Lady Louis often entertained and many guests would come to Brook House or in a more leisurely nature to Adsdean, the lovely country mansion the Mountbattens rented near Chichester. It was there that the weekends were spent. Set high on the Sussex Downs, the eighteenth-century house occupied a commanding position, with the grounds incorporating a private golf course and a polo pitch too – Lord Louis was a keen polo player and he stabled many ponies there that he trained for the sport.

Normally, I would drive with Lady Louis from London to Adsdean on Friday nights, leaving His Lordship to make his own way from Portsmouth. We would return in the grey Rolls-Royce on Monday mornings to Brook House, where social gatherings were inclined to be more formal.

Brook House boasted a very splendid ballroom with white marble walls and crystal chandeliers. It was approached by a marble stairway and gilt balustrade. Some dazzling, spectacular nights were staged in the ballroom, often with King George V and Queen Mary present, along with other members of the Royal family and the élite of the thirties society.

Identifying Royal faces was an essential part of my duties, but there were moments of catastrophe. One morning a gentleman in a dark blue overcoat arrived at the front door without an appointment and was questioned as to his purpose by Fred Reed, who was Lord Louis' footman.

'I have come to see Her Ladyship,' declared the stranger.

'Who shall I say is calling, Sir?' he asked.

'Mr Edward,' replied our visitor.

Fred passed me in the hall with a suspicious glint in his eye. One never called on the Mountbattens without an appointment. Disturbing Her Ladyship in the drawing room, he said, 'There is a Mr

Edward at the door to see you, m'Lady . . . only he doesn't appear to have an appointment.'

'Mr Edward?' said Her Ladyship curiously. 'I don't think . . .' She was interrupted by the stranger, who had swept into the house, brushing me aside, and was peering into the room.

'Yes, it's me Edwina,' he said, while Fred turned on his heel ready to protect Her Ladyship from the intruder if necessary. Her Ladyship laughed and greeted 'Mr Edward' with a warm embrace. It was none other than the Prince of Wales! Fred and I shrank from the room in embarrassment.

I was to be involved in a similar incident with the Prince of Wales some weeks later. At the time we were being pestered by a hoax caller who would ring through to Brook House on various pretexts. Refusing to accept he had dialled a private number, he would insist that we were the zoo, the hospital, the gas works, or whatever. I became increasingly angry with the hoaxer and after a spate of endless pestering I thought I would well and truly deal with him on his next call.

The telephone rang and a voice I now regarded as familiar said, 'This is the Prince of Wales.'

'Look,' I said irritably, 'I've had enough of you. If you don't stop making these ridiculous calls I shall get the police to trace you.' I slammed down the receiver, not stopping to think until it was too late that it just might have been the Prince of Wales.

Alas, it was, and His Royal Highness did not hesitate to convey his vexed feelings to Her Ladyship. Hauled on to the mat, I humbly explained about the stream of hoax calls. Her Ladyship was forgiving and said, 'Don't worry, Charles, I'll square things with the Prince of Wales. I am sure he will understand.'

When His Royal Highness next came to the house, he singled me out and joked about the episode.

'I don't blame you for censoring Her Ladyship's calls, Charles,' he said, 'but what bounder would say he was the Prince of Wales?'

Another popular visitor to the Mountbattens was Prince George, the Duke of Kent, who rarely missed the weekend house parties at Adsdean, where we had at least a dozen guest bedrooms. The Duke had many little idiosyncrasies. Sleeping in a different coloured pyjama top to his trousers was one of them and when I laid out his bedclothes this would often confuse me.

The Duke was guarded by a ferocious Alsatian named Tessa who would not allow anyone into his room, but I managed to make friends with the dog and eventually gained her trust to the extent where she would allow me to take her for a morning run while the Duke was having his bath.

I had been with Lord and Lady Louis for only seventeen months when His Lordship was appointed Fleet Wireless Officer to the Mediterranean Fleet which was based in Malta, and this meant a move for the entire household. By now the children had a new nanny – Nanny Gifford who had taken over from Nanny Woodard on her retirement. I was asked to escort Miss Pamela and Miss Patricia, together with their nanny, to Malta. We were booked aboard a P.&O. liner which ironically was called the *Viceroy of India*.

We sailed from Tilbury in September and we had not been many hours out of port when a gale blew up. We were in for a very rough trip. The ship pitched and rolled like a log and most of the passengers were sick. Fortunately I was not affected and neither, more remarkably, was Miss Patricia, whose cheerful alertness won her the deck 'tote' for guessing the ship's mileage over two twenty-four-hour spans. Most passengers were glad of a respite in Gibraltar before our journey continued to Malta in calmer seas.

Lord and Lady Louis had gone on ahead, and they were waiting to greet us in Valletta when the ship anchored in the glistening blue waters, the sun blazing down on us from a clear sky.

The Mountbattens had occupied a spacious villa, the Casa Medina, perched high on a hill overlooking Valletta harbour. The house was typically Mediterranean in its design, and its gardens were very beautiful with a profusion of flowers still in blossom.

Things had been well organized. Lord and Lady Louis had been given use of the *Lizard*, which belonged to Lady Louis' sister, Lady Delamere. The green-hulled *Lizard* was well known in Maltese waters. She was 66 feet long, and sleek not only in looks but in performance too, with a top speed of thirty-two knots produced by her twin 1,000 h.p. engines. There were cabins to accommodate six guests, and there were berths for the skipper, Captain Warpole, and his crew. Room was found for me and two other members of the household staff whenever we went to sea. The galley was well equipped and in the absence of a cook I was appointed ship's chef on many of the weekends we set sail.

These were peaceful, halcyon days and the happiness of Lord and Lady Louis, with their infants around them, generated a warmth that embraced all those in their employ. This feeling of family unity remained even when m'Lord and Lady pursued their own separate activities.

Life was as much a quest for Lady Louis as it was for His Lordship. When Lord Louis sailed with the Mediterranean Fleet on various exercises, it was customary for Lady Louis to embark on her own travels. She once set out with her sister-in-law, Lady Milford Haven, on a danger-prone expedition to Syria, Iraq, Transjordania and Iran, travelling by whatever means possible. His Lordship admired his wife's enterprising spirit and he would listen with keen interest to her experiences which she would vividly recount on her return.

Malta created so much joy for us all at that time. The Maltese were such a friendly people and the island with its quaint churches and natural rural beauty became a second home for many of us.

It would always be a red letter day when the Mediterranean Fleet sailed from the Grand Harbour with its flotilla of battleships, aircraft carriers, submarines, destroyers and other frigates. It was always a moving and impressive sight.

I would stand on the cliffs and distinguish Lord Louis' ship, H.M.S. *Daring*. I had been aboard on many occasions to ensure that His Lordship's clothes and uniforms were in good order. His Lordship would sometimes communicate with me from his ship by signal. One morning he sent a signal enquiring, 'Where is my tie clip?'

I replied through the Naval wireless operator, 'Your 0830 [the time his signal was transmitted] is in your top pocket.'

I quickly got to know the Naval abbreviations; the traditional R.S.V.P. would sometimes warrant an M.R.U. (Much Regret Unable)!

During these Malta days, and when Lord and Lady Louis were

fortunate enough to both be at home, the Casa Medina saw many of their favourite guests. Not least among them was Mr Noel Coward, who was the toast of London's West End. Mr Coward had been a frequent visitor to Adsdean and he made a tremendous impact on the staff when he appeared in Malta. His dry sense of humour and sardonic attitude to life accentuated his sartorial flamboyance. He had a penchant for reefer jackets, cravats and extravagant cigarette holders. His musical talents seemed to be inspired by the blossom-scented surroundings of the Casa Medina and he requisitioned the grand piano in the lounge to compose a new West End score. I took him in a cocktail one evening. He was scribbling notes on to a scrap of sheet music, much of which was strewn on top of the piano.

.'Charles,' he said, 'listen to this and tell me what you think.'

He played three or four chords and turned to me to study my reaction.

'It sounds very catchy, Sir,' I said.

'Ah,' said Mr Coward, 'we're a long way from being finished yet. His Lordship fights his battles on the bridge of his ship. Mine are here at the keyboard, Charles, and I think I would rather have it that way. It's much safer.'

In a day or two Mr Coward had finished one of the songs of his new score. It was entitled 'Mad Dogs and Englishmen Go Out In the Mid-day Sun' and he sang the lyrics at the top of his voice, unabashed by the presence of other guests in the house and encouraged through it all by Lord and Lady Louis. This particular song became one of his best known and before Mr Coward left Malta we were all humming it.

Some years later he based his film *In Which We Serve* on the exploits of His Lordship's famous destroyer H.M.S. *Kelly* which Lord Louis captained into the Second World War.

Many European monarchs also came to visit us in Malta. His Lordship's cousin, King Alfonso of Spain, was thrown into a quandary when his own personal valet fell and broke an ankle.

'I don't like asking you to double up on your duties, Charles, but is there anything you can do?' asked Lord Louis.

I rearranged my usual routine so that I could take care of his needs.

'This is very kind of you, Charles,' said the King, who spoke good English.

His Majesty stayed with us for several weeks and every morning, when I took in his breakfast tray, he would enquire as to the state of the morning's weather. Without hesitation I would say, 'It's lovely and sunny, Your Majesty,' as the weather in Malta never seemed to vary. I'm afraid I became rather parrot-like. One morning the usual assurance of sunny weather had just rolled off my tongue when I pulled the curtains to discover, to my horror, that it was raining with all the rage of a monsoon! His Majesty burst into laughter.

Sudden storms of this kind were rare in Malta, but when they occurred heavy seas would whip up and shipping would scurry to port for safety. Usually they did not last for long and blue skies would quickly return. The climate, overall, was ideal. The heat was never too oppressive and the children loved it. Miss Pamela and Miss Patricia were suntanned and Nanny Gifford looked a healthy picture too. Pleasant hours would be spent watching divers recovering pennies tossed for fun into the deeper rock pools along the coastline.

We all went swimming every day – including the other 'member' of our family, a pet terrier named Bimbo that Lady Louis had given me, having been presented with the dog by Hurlingham Polo Club. Bimbo refused to be left at home, especially when he detected that an outing was in the air!

The family kept Sealyhams and one of them – Tops'l – nearly got me the sack because his affections were aligned more with me than his Lordship! It hurt Lord Louis' feelings and he threatened: 'If you don't discourage Tops'l from following you everywhere, then he'll have to go – or you will!'

Lord and Lady Louis' passion for animals went much further than the inclination to be surrounded by household pets and in the years ahead my duties as footman and valet took on a new dimension.

Even in Malta they adopted a honey bear they named Rastas who was an absolute bundle of mischief. When he was only two and a half feet tall he was very cuddly and one could manage him easily, but of course he quickly grew. He was allowed to run freely about the house and Lord Louis would love to play with him at the end of the day when he returned from duty. Occasionally they fell out, like the day Lord Louis had some Naval top brass over for lunch, and Rastas, scampering between their legs in the dining room, got his marching orders.

Rastas wasn't amused. He wasn't going to accept being locked out of the house – not by a long chalk. He started digging by the front door and actually burrowed his way back into the house, upturning the floor tiles in the process as he emerged in the hall. His Lordship gasped with astonishment.

'Rastas!' he roared, as the bear scrambled from the hole and scurried into the house . . . but Rastas wasn't really listening. He had taken refuge under a carpet.

'Charles!' bawled His Lordship. 'Come and capture Rastas before he tears the place to pieces!'

I went and gathered Rastas from under the carpet and rebuked him. He put a paw to his mouth as he always did when he felt any shame.

At sunset, after his Naval colleagues had gone, Lord Louis' conscience troubled him. He expressed the feeling that he had been too hard on Rastas.

'I think I upset him,' he said, 'what shall I do?'

'I am sure he will forgive you, m'Lord, if you give him an egg to play with,' I suggested.

'An egg?'

I produced one from the kitchen and gave it to Rastas in front of Lord Louis. Rastas rolled on his back in glee and cracked the egg with the finesse of an expert. Then he poured the yoke into his mouth and instantly began chattering with pleasure. His Lordship was fascinated, and thereafter he made a habit of keeping an egg in his desk drawer for Rastas.

In time, however, Rastas grew too big for any of us to manage and we had to part with him. He went to the Whale Island Zoo at Portsmouth where other pets that Lord and Lady Louis 'adopted' eventually found their homes.

In the meantime, Lord Louis' Naval career was flourishing. In 1932 he was promoted to the rank of commander. In 1933 he returned to England.

I think Lord Louis was determined that I should find my sea legs. When it was time to leave Malta, he arranged for my passage home sleeping in a cabin that was actually situated on the crow's nest of another of His Majesty's ships, the *Resolution*. It was a long climb to bed every night and a hair-raising descent in the mornings for breakfast with the Naval deckhands!

My dog Bimbo returned with me and he was found a comfortable niche on the deck, but on reaching Portsmouth he was promptly placed into quarantine, where he was isolated for four months. Poor Bimbo. I am afraid he came to a ghastly end. Back in England he chased a water rat into a frozen pond and drowned beneath the ice. I was very upset and so were Lord and Lady Louis when they heard of our lovable dog's sad misadventure.

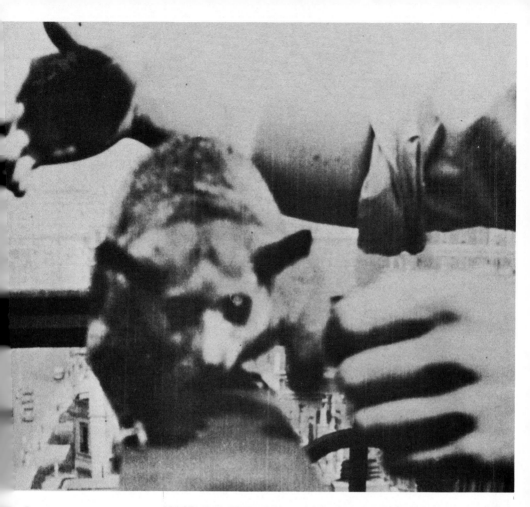

: Bozo the bush baby
g loose on the penthouse
Lord and Lady Louis'
ane home in London

Rastas on the vine trellis
Medina in Malta

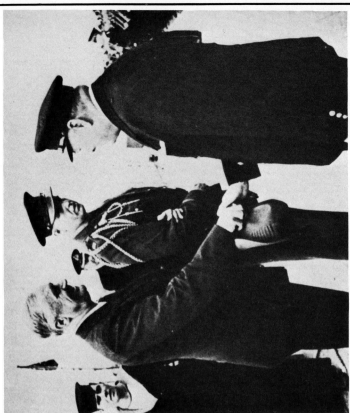

"ATLANTIC MEETING"

WITH THE BEST OF GOOD WISHES

FOR

CHRISTMAS AND THE NEW YEAR

from

Edwina and Louis Mountbatten

Christmas 1941. Lord Louis' note refers to the Maltese stewards who were on board H.M.S. *Kelly* with him

3

On the Bus with Prince Philip

During our two years overseas great changes had been made at Brook House. Indeed, it was no longer Brook House as we remembered it. The original house had been demolished and a modern block of flats over a car showroom now stood in its place.

Lord and Lady Louis kept the penthouse, on the eighth floor, and they also retained the floor below, though they didn't actually live there until 1936. Both floors opened up on to their own private garden balconies, overlooking Hyde Park in one direction and Marble Arch in the other. There was still ample room for entertaining and a private lift served the two floors.

Unfortunately, the newly-installed lift, which Lord Louis helped to design, was acting temperamentally on the morning our first guest, Queen Mary, arrived. Decorators still working on the modernizations were upsetting the button controls, although I was not aware of this when I conducted Her Majesty into the lift. Neither was Lord Louis who accompanied Her Majesty on the ascent!

Up and down the lift soared like a yo-yo, much to the consternation of Lord Louis. There was nothing I could do! But Her Majesty was not upset by the experience and regarded it as something of a novelty. When the lift doors finally opened on the eighth floor, she exclaimed, 'I enjoyed that. We haven't got anything like this at Buckingham Palace! I will have to ask His Majesty to see if we can get one.'

This automation of the staircase put an end to the traditional assembly of the household staff at the front door; they were usually posted there *en masse* whenever Royalty was expected. But His Lordship persisted with this unnecessary formality at Adsdean and frankly I got hot under the collar about it to the point where I decided we would have to have a showdown.

Abruptly one evening I fired the first salvo.

'When you're keeping watch on the bridge of your ship, you don't have all your crew standing up there with you,' I remonstrated to His Lordship, 'otherwise there would be no one left in the engine room to answer your bloody orders!'

His Lordship's expression was incredulous. For an agonizing moment I thought I had overstepped the mark. Then he nodded, 'Charles, you are quite right. In future we will only have one footman on duty in the hall; the rest of the staff will get on with their normal duties.'

His Lordship's understanding, and willingness, to listen and reasonably accept another point of view forged that very special working relationship between us where I was permitted free expression, even if it was critical or perhaps distasteful.

I acknowledged His Lordship's position; and he acknowledged mine. We held each other in mutual respect. It did not waiver through fifty years. I knew that His Lordship would not have tolerated an ingratiating 'yes' man as a servant. He secretly admired the way I held my ground and spoke my mind. I was always conscious of the fact that he held the whip hand, but I suppose I gambled on his leniency because it was clearly not a trait of his character to pull rank. Neither was he the kind of man to bear malice. One day's argument would be buried and forgotten by the next morning.

If Lord Louis thought, on hindsight, that he was wrong then it was not beneath his dignity to apologize to me. It was one of his most endearing qualities. By the same token, if I felt I had acted in haste and expressed one word too many, then I would also make my peace with him. It was rare for a complete stalemate to occur, but when it did, then the strategy would be one of compromise.

Sometimes, our rows would cause consternation, especially among other servants and members of the family. But in the end they eventually came to regard us like two old warriors who could sort out their own battles! Even Lady Louis would let us get on with it and when the air was clear she would say, 'Thank goodness you've got that out of your systems!' She would never take sides, unless she could see a humourous aspect.

Sometimes, I think Lord Louis used me as a 'sounding board' when he devised time- and labour-saving ideas for the house, because he would ask me what I thought, even when I suspected he had already made a decision.

That I had gained Lord Louis' trust was evident to me when he asked if I would mind assisting his mother, the Dowager Marchioness of Milford Haven, when a sudden flux of guests descended on her at Kensington Palace.

My 'lease loan' was to span four months, but I told Lord Louis it would be a great honour, and subsequently I moved into the Palace, occupying a small room only two or three doors away from the Marchioness's chamber.

It was 1934 – the year of the Duke of Kent's marriage to one of the loveliest of Europe's princesses, Marina of Greece and Denmark. Most of the Marchioness's expected guests were coming to London for the wedding, but my real charge at the Palace, and indeed at Adsdean over the coming months, was her lively and adventurous grandson Philip who had been sent to England by his mother for his schooling.

Prince Philip was then just thirteen years of age, an inquisitive youngster whose fresh, innocent complexion rather belied his imaginative and carefree spirit, which was not to desert him in later life! Thanks to His Royal Highness no one could suggest our monarchy lacked verve, and these characteristics were truly ingrained in him as a youngster.

I tried not to speculate on the plots he must have hatched at Cheam Preparatory School, but I know that at Kensington Palace the patience of Grandmama was sometimes a little exhausted by his restless, enquiring nature. She would always keep a good eye on him, tidying up behind him and ensuring his clothes were in good order, but inevitably she needed breathing space to collect her own thoughts. That's where I came in.

'Charles,' she said one afternoon, 'would you mind taking Philip off to the cinema? I know he is dying to go, but I don't think I could sit through it with him.'

Prince Philip caught my eye and the plea on his face made it impossible for me to refuse.

'I think you'll enjoy it too, Charles,' he said.

'What are we going to see?' I asked.

'*Treasure Island*,' he rejoined.

'Yes,' said the Marchioness, 'I think that will be very suitable.'

An outing to the cinema became a regular treat. The Marchioness would give me six shillings, sufficient money for our seats and a tray of tea during the interval, and enough, too, for our bus fares home.

Prince Philip's passion for adventure was reflected in his choice of films. I recall that we saw two seafaring epics, one of them *Mutiny on the Bounty* with Charles Laughton, which I am sure would have sewn the seeds for the young Prince's Naval career if a romantic vision had not already been conjured by the salty tales spun by Uncle Dickie!

Some of the swashbuckling exploits of the screen also rubbed off on Prince Philip, who once purloined a collection of 'Reserved' notices from the Victoria Metropole, in those days the most popular cinema in London. Aware that I wasn't watching him as closely as I should have been, His Royal Highness distributed them on the seats of the open top deck of our bus home, much to the bewilderment of newly-boarding passengers.

Soon the conductor was on hand, looking suspiciously at my young charge.

'What's going on here?' he demanded, pointing at one of the 'Reserved' placards.

Recognizing its origin, I accepted responsibility.

'We're lucky the conductor didn't tell us to walk home the rest of the way!' I said sternly to the young Prince.

Prince Philip's only concern was that I shouldn't tell his Grandmama.

'You won't split, Charles, will you?' he pleaded. 'I promise I will return them to the cinema when we go next week.'

I thought Prince Philip would now tuck the placards out of sight. But I was wrong. He made further use of them, tying them to the doorhandles of guest rooms in Kensington Palace! He was in his element to see the confusion his little ruse caused the important wedding guests!

Every morning Prince Philip and his cousin Lady Tatiana, who was two years older but who shared his zest for living, would come to the pantry and play a game of darts with the staff. Some mornings I would partner Prince Philip and the chauffeur would pair up with Lady Tatiana and we would have many spectacular bull's eye championships. I was always careful to protect the two youngsters from rebounding darts; if they had suffered any injury I would not have relished the prospect of facing Grandmama or Uncle Dickie!

As it was, I took the blame when Prince Philip ripped his best school trousers when playing football with the servants in the stable yard at Adsdean.

'Charles, it's all your damned fault,' glowered His Lordship unjustly. 'Why did you allow him to play football in his best school pants? You had better get on and mend them. He'll want them by the morning.'

When Prince Philip went to bed, I took his trousers to my room and darned them with a needle and yarn supplied by one of the maids. They really needed professional invisible mending, but I did my best and Prince Philip didn't even give them a glance. Like all boys of that age, he wasn't worried how scagged his pants were.

Prince Philip was always in the thick of the action and one of the popular improvised games at Adsdean was 'bicycle polo' in which Philip managed to entice Uncle Dickie into playing with us. Uncle Dickie's polo sticks would be chopped down to an appropriate size for the bicycle version and we would mark out a pitch on one of the fairways of the golf course. Even His Lordship's trained polo team members would love to become embroiled in the thrills and spills that came with more profusion from the saddle of a bicycle than perhaps from their ponies!

Prince Philip was pretty adept at the sport, weaving in and out between the older cyclists, and he often emerged as the day's highest goal-scorer.

Lord Louis remarked, 'If His Highness can come to ride a horse as well as a bicycle he will make a fine polo player.'

His nephew was to justify that prediction in the years ahead when he was to emulate his Uncle Dickie at Cowdray Park, Windsor, Cirencester and other polo haunts across the country.

From the early thirties His Lordship had been a keen polo player and later wrote a book on the sport called *Introduction to Polo* under the pseudonym 'Marco'. Among the 'regulars' in his team were Commander Lamb, Major Robert Neville and Commander Teddy Hayward-Lonsdale. Lord Louis played for both 'The Shrimps', his own private team, and the 'Bluejackets', the Navy's team, and we would often transport six polo ponies to Deauville for matches against the French. Twice Lord Louis fell and broke a collar-bone. His mother, who had watched both matches, shook her head and said, 'I don't think I had better come to watch you again, Dickie. I bring you bad luck!'

There was hardly the opportunity for me to take up polo, but from time to time I would go out riding with Lord Louis' string of ponies when they were being exercised in the mornings.

I saw less of Prince Philip when he departed for further schooling at Gordonstoun, but he still came down to Adsdean for his vacations. Because of the constant activity there, it always held considerable fascination for him.

I would have liked to have encouraged Philip and his Uncle Dickie more into the ways of golf, but they much preferred polo and riding. However, His Lordship would swing a club or two, and Lady Louis was also quite keen, and throughout the season various golf tournaments would be staged on the Adsdean course. Ultimately, His Lordship's interest declined and he considered stopping playing altogether because I was winning too many of the trophies!

'I think we had better devise a tournament where you're the only competitor, Charles!' he would grumble.

When we returned to Malta for another two-year spell, Lady Louis, full of pioneering spirit, flew into Valletta in a two-seater seaplane that was so advanced in design that it might have been a worthy competitor for the Schneider Cup. Her Ladyship squatted in the cockpit behind the pilot, having taken any necessary cosmetics and clothes in a small vanity case that only just found space in the fuselage.

Once more I had travelled by sea, humping the luggage with me and loading it on to a horse-drawn cart on reaching Malta for its despatch to the Casa Medina, the villa we were again to occupy. My love for Malta had not waned and the days passed as blissfully as before.

His Lordship was on duty with the Mediterranean Fleet from dawn to dusk but however much work he absorbed, he always made light of it. Even when he fell sick with jaundice he was prepared to work on, but the rising fever overtook him. All his engagements had to be cancelled for three weeks. His pyjamas and bedsheets needed changing almost every other hour and I shared the bedside duties with Arthur Rutherford, one of the footmen.

Eventually the fever passed and Lord Louis slowly recovered. But no sooner was he well than I developed similar symptoms. I was taken sick during the Fleet's water sports regatta. We were on board one of the yachts, and feeling suddenly groggy I had to go below deck where I crumpled up on a couch. Lady Louis followed me down and, like the nurse she was, she lifted my head on to her lap and stroked my brow as it began to perspire from the rushing fever.

'You've caught this from His Lordship,' sympathized Lady Louis. 'Don't worry, Charles, we will soon get you better.'

A signal was sent back to shore and a doctor was awaiting my arrival on the quayside. I was driven straight back to the house where he diagnosed jaundice. Fortunately, my attack was not as bad as Lord Louis' and I was back on my feet again within a matter of ten days.

His Lordship was always trying to entice me out to sea on an exercise and he finally succeeded aboard the H.M.S. *Wishart*, his second command, after H.M.S. *Daring*. He assured me we would be out of Valletta for only three days. They turned out to be the most traumatic three days of my stay in Malta as the moment we lost sight of land we ran into a frightening storm.

I was with His Lordship on the bridge and I made an excuse to go to my cabin to get some seasickness pills. By the time I had got to my cabin the ship was running into the full force of the storm and the order was given to batten down all hatches. I found the pills and hastened to return to Lord Louis, but I found I was locked in! No one could hear me banging on the door.

As the ship recoiled from the impact of the huge waves battering its decks, I was thrown to the floor and I lay there until the storm abated. A seaman finally opened my door and I stumbled out feeling distinctly queasy. There was a twinkle in Lord Louis' eyes when he saw me re-appear.

'Where have you been, Charles? You missed all the fun,' he said, and then, noticing my peaky colour, he added, 'Didn't you take your pills?'

I reached for the rail.

It was summer when we again returned to England. We spent many gorgeous days at Adsdean, as usual entertaining a constant stream of guests. By this time even the most famous of our guests had to compete with the resident 'attractions'. These included a lion cub, christened Sabi, that Lady Louis had brought back with her from Africa and had thrust into my arms at Southampton.

'Charles,' cried Her Ladyship excitedly, 'here is someone else for you to look after!'

I grabbed hold of Sabi and wondered how long it would be before we would open our own zoological garden. We were emptying the jungles of the world. A pair of wallabies from Australia had been settled on us, there was the mongoose who would wrap itself around Miss Pamela's neck like a fox furtail, Rastas the bear, and next we inherited Bozo, a bush baby, who became the favourite scamp of them all! Domestic pets might have taken second place had it not been for Her Ladyship's three Sealyham dogs whose leader Mizzen had no intention of losing out on the spotlight of attention.

The bizarre antics of our four-legged friends were always able to steal the show, as screen idols Douglas Fairbanks and Mary Pickford uncomplainingly experienced, while Charlie Chaplin conceded, 'It's true, you know. Never work with animals!'

I remember Mr Chaplin's very first call on the Mountbattens at home. He came to Brook House and I was absolutely mesmerized to find myself confronting the famous silent screen star on the doorstep one morning.

'Are Lord and Lady Mountbatten at home?' he said.

Having seen his films without a word passing his lips, I recoiled in shock on hearing his voice for the first time. It was clear and articulate. Although I did not realize it then, he was very close to Lord and Lady Louis, having made a film in Hollywood with them, a 'home' movie he entitled *Nice and Friendly*, presenting it for private screening for the enjoyment of the family and their friends. In the picture Charlie Chaplin, playing his familiar role, was seen ambushing Lord Louis' valet Mr Thorogood and beating him over the head with a hammer!

'Take caution, Charles,' winked Lord Louis on my first viewing of the movie, 'you can see what will happen to you if you stay with us!'

Having now met Mr Chaplin in the flesh, the thing that struck me most about him was that he really did wear his famous bowler hat, and carried a cane too. But the moustache was noticeably absent in real life and instead of a tatty jacket and baggy trousers, he wore the most elegant of pinstripe suits that made him look like a City stockbroker. We worried in case his clothes became torn or spoiled by our animals, who vied for affection from all our callers.

Sabi, the lion cub, loved to gnaw other people's shoes, and Lord Louis' slippers were a nightly target. He would disappear with them and hole up under the bed for a nourishing chew. Lord Louis was in the habit of hiding his slippers from Sabi because of this, but one evening he forgot where he put them and came to blame the lion cub once more.

'Charles,' he yelled when he came home and reclined into his favourite armchair, 'where are my slippers? That bloody lion has pinched them again.'

'No, m'Lord,' I said, 'Sabi is in my room and he hasn't got them, I can assure you. Didn't you put them away?'

'Dammit you're right, Charles,' sighed Lord Louis, 'but where in the hell have I hidden them?''

We searched for hours but it wasn't until the next morning that I found the slippers – on top of the closet.

Sabi was highly intelligent and he would actually follow me on to the golf course and squat like a dog whenever I paused to take my shot from the green. He grew quite big and eventually came to occupy one of the horse boxes at Adsdean.

His appetite was always keen and when our local butcher delivered a huge order of prime Scottish beef for a banquet being prepared for King Alfonso, then Sabi applied the laws of the jungle! He raided the open-backed van while the butcher was in the kitchen, and naturally made away with the juiciest joint, the King's joint! The butcher, emerging into the yard, caught sight of Sabi as he made off across the estate and could not believe his eyes.

He rushed back into the house and cried, 'You're not going to believe this, but a lion has stolen the meat from the back of my van!'

We all quietly smiled at one another. We knew precisely who the culprit was.

'We had better get after him,' I said.

The butcher was almost dumbstruck.

'Are you crazy?' he said, panic-stricken, 'I tell you it was a lion. You had better call the police.'

We laughed. 'That's only Sabi,' I said, 'he's just a cub.'

Lord Louis was highly amused when the incident was related to him and the butcher was compensated for the loss of his meat, including the replacement joint he had to bring in time for the King's dinner.

Sabi's greatest fans were of course Miss Pamela and Miss Patricia. They loved his company and they would prance around the estate with him until, like Rastas, he became too much to manage and had to go to the Whale Island Zoo.

But it was Bozo, the bush baby, who really came to steal everyone's affections. It was not unusual for me to drop by on Lord Louis' room and find His Lordship engaged in an animated conversation with Bozo.

'I get a lot more sense out of Bozo than I do from one or two people I could name!' he ruminated.

Bozo also became a firm favourite of Princess Elizabeth and Princess Margaret, who as youngsters would come to Brook House to play with Miss Patricia and Miss Pamela.

By any stretch of the imagination I could not have realized that

Princess Elizabeth would one day become Queen, and yet those refined, dignified qualities the world recognizes in Her Majesty today were perceptible in her character even at that young age. When she was eight years old she was already a pretty girl with dark, curly hair and, I thought, the image of her father, then the Duke of York.

The two sets of sisters mixed well together and they would plot all sorts of games. Often I was the victim of their conspiracies! I remember Miss Patricia, who was the eldest of the four, would send me on an errand while staging a raid to release Bozo from his cage, which was kept in my room. The Royal children's faces lit up whenever this little ploy succeeded; getting Bozo out to play was a favourite pastime.

As for Bozo, he enjoyed every rip-roaring minute! He had developed into a real scatterbrain, capsizing lamps, bowls, chairs and tables in the house and swinging from chandeliers and picture rails. He would impishly tug Mizzen, the Sealyham's, whiskers, and then run for his life, ascending curtains and door frames, or take refuge on the convenient shoulders of one of the children, which they particularly encouraged.

My one warning to them was to ensure they closed all the windows because Bozo never missed a chance to escape and I spent many precarious afternoons on the roof trying to lure him back into the house. He didn't usually respond until darkness – and the temperature – fell!

Wherever and whenever the family travelled, then Bozo went too, even to the most distant places. The airlines came to treat him like a V.I.P. His cage was stowed on the flight deck, near Lord Louis' feet.

I can still visualize the astonished faces in the hotel foyer in New York when Bozo, chattering away merrily in his cage, was checked in and stacked atop the baggage for the bell captain to take up to Lord and Lady Louis' suite.

'Can I ask you something?' the puzzled bell captain said, tugging my arm, 'are all you English so crazy? I've heard of folk taking away their dog or their cat on holiday, but a monkey . . .?'

'It's not a monkey,' I said, 'it's a bush baby.'

'Yeah?' said the bell captain. 'You watch out it ain't a gorilla!'

For Lord and Lady Louis it was a private visit to New York and they spent several days sightseeing, leaving Bozo in my charge.

'We're going to the top of the Empire State Building,' announced His Lordship one morning, 'and we just can't take Bozo. If he escaped up there I don't know what would happen.'

Sadly, the trip did result in Bozo's death, but not in a fall from the Empire State Building as Lord Louis feared. We had moved on to our next stopover in Jamaica and there Lord Louis went for massage treatment. Bozo's inquisitive nature was too much, he swallowed the contents of a bottle of liniment! It was, alas, his undoing. He became ill, and on board the homeward-bound liner, the *Queen Mary*, his condition worsened. When we got back to Brook House I immediately called the veterinary surgeon at London Zoo.

The vet was quickly with us, but it was too late. Poor Bozo died minutes before he arrived. The cause of his death was diagnosed as congestion of the lungs as a result of drinking the poisonous liniment.

Miss Patricia and Miss Pamela sobbed; so did we all. Bozo had really been one of the family; his spirit had been irrepressible.

4
Putting a Zip In It!

Lord Louis, inventor of many brilliant navigational and signal devices during his distinguished Naval career, was to take a step forward for mankind that would truly identify him as a pioneer!

It was the mid-thirties, the age of the domestic zip – an item that fascinated Lord Louis, who believed, with remarkable vision, that it could be put to a more functional use. Giving great thought to the affair, he adapted it as a trouser zip; a brainwave, I am sure, that earned him the silent thanks of millions of men across the world, even though His Lordship's motives may have been entirely selfish. Lord Louis simply detested the fuss buttons caused.

'They stitch the damn things on in such stupid places and there is invariably one that is missing or hanging loose,' His Lordship would lament.

Lord Louis – a man whose wardrobe consisted of never less than thirty different robes of high office – believed that time spent on dressing was too precious to waste.

'A minute can be as costly as an hour,' he would chide me if his clothes weren't precisely laid out ready for him to wear when he went to change.

His Lordship set about streamlining the process. All his shirts came to be designed with collars attached – even the stiff-winged creations he wore for ceremonial functions. He adopted turnover socks that cut away at the calf so that suspenders were dispensed with; he favoured slip-on, elasticated shoes so that he didn't have to bother tying laces; he kept braces for his Mess and evening dress, but had them permanently stitched to the trousers; and he would wear a buttonless waistcoat which pulled over his head like a jumper.

Lord Louis' ingenuity knew no bounds. In later months he devised a 'Simplex' shirt with built in Y-fronts that he could slide into like a stretch suit. I am sure that if he had not become an Admiral he would have made a superb clothes designer, to which future trouser-zip manufacturers would surely have testified.

Everything that Lord Louis did was intended for practical use and with all his time-saving sartorial aids, His Lordship could bath and change inside two minutes. We didn't exactly put a stop watch on it but we found we could accomplish this feat one night when His Lordship was dashing out for an important dinner engagement at Buckingham Palace. His arrival home at Brook House was only five minutes before he was due at the Palace and if there was one obsession that Lord Louis had it was on the matter of punctuality. He could not bear to be late; and neither would he tolerate anyone else being late if the appointment was with him!

'Charles,' he said, flying through the door that particular night, 'I've got to be downstairs in two minutes for the car.'

'Don't worry, m'Lord, you will make it.'

His bath was run, and casting off his clothes in a pile on the floor he slithered into the water like a seal. Then, while he dried his chest, I took another towel to dry his back. His fresh clothes were ready for him and thanks to the Simplex shirt, the roll-on waistcoat and the slip-on shoes, Lord Louis was immaculately on his way down to the waiting car within the time limit he had set.

Lord Louis liked to be fashionably dressed, but there was a period in the thirties when he fell behind modern-day style, which became transparently clear on a visit to America where he was to inspect a U.S. Naval base. We were in Miami changing planes when a U.S. Naval equerry mistook me for Lord Louis, as he considered I was more distinctly dressed!

'Where do you think the old man wants his luggage put?' asked the Naval aide, nudging Lord Louis.

Lord Louis raised his eyebrows.

'My valet is over there,' he told the sailor. 'Please ask him. He knows precisely what to do.'

Poor Lord Louis, dressed in an unflattering grey flannel suit that he insisted on wearing, could not get over the shock of being mistaken for the valet. Peeved by the incident, he told Lady Louis what had happened.

'Edwina, what do you think? That wretched fellow thought I was the valet!'

Her Ladyship took one look at her husband and said, 'Dickie, the way you're dıessed, I'm not surprised. That's a dreadful suit you're wearing.'

Lord Louis, now feeling conscious about his dress, asked me to unpack another suit from one of the cases. We were in the airport lounge and as discreetly as possible I managed to fish out something else, advising Lord Louis to change in the gentlemen's 'Rest Room'.

When he re-appeared in a dark, pinstripe suit, Lady Louis gave her approval. 'That's much better, Dickie.'

There was one snag, which I'm sure didn't occur to Lord or Lady Louis at the time. While His Lordship was changing, our luggage had been loaded on the plane and I was left holding the grey flannel suit. The Naval aide was looking at it and I caught his gaze, reading what was going through his mind.

'Yes,' I said, 'you're about His Lordship's size. Here, please take it.'

That might well have been the end of the episode, except that a few months later, back in England, I walked into Lord Louis' room one morning and enquired what he would like to wear that day.

'I think I will put on my grey flannel suit, Charles, if you can get it out for me,' he replied.

I didn't quite know what to say and His Lordship caught my quizzical expression.

'What's the matter, Charles? Why are you looking so agitated?' said His Lordship.

'Well, m'Lord,' I spluttered, trying to gather courage, 'I'm sorry, the grey flannel suit may be difficult to find.'

'Why, in heaven's name?' said Lord Louis, his voice darkening.

'It's like this, m'Lord,' I said, taking the bull by the horns, 'when we were in Miami that time I gave the suit away to that American Naval aide who helped us at the airport. Our luggage had gone and I didn't quite know what to do with the suit.'

Lord Louis slapped a hand to his forehead in disbelief and cried out, 'Edwina! Come quickly!'

Her Ladyship came rushing through wondering what had happened.

'What's wrong, Dickie?' she cried, fearing the worst.

'It's my grey flannel suit. You know the one. What do you think? Charles gave it away in Miami!'

Lady Louis' face lit up. She turned to me and said, 'Congratulations, Charles! That's the best day's work you've ever done!'

It seemed to be an appropriate moment for me to persuade His Lordship to come into line with fashion trends, and having now acquired the support of his wife, I began to bully him into changing his tailor.

I grumbled at His Lordship, 'You've got to do something about it, m'Lord. Your present tailors are not keeping up with the times. Every suit they make for you is a disaster. They all make you look "bottle-necked". They're not right on you at all.'

His Lordship surrendered.

'All right, Charles,' he said to placate me, 'let's try someone else. Who do you suggest I go to?'

At that period many celebrities and film stars – the people who created the trends in London – were dressed by Hawes and Curtis and I recommended them to His Lordship although I had had no earlier dealings with them.

His Lordship agreed we should give them a try and said, 'Let's really find out just how good they are. Let's ask them to make a tail coat and evening dress. That should put them to the test.'

I approached the company and got some pattern books. One of their tailors came along to measure Lord Louis and over the next two weeks he had three fittings before the order was ready.

Lord Louis thought he would stage a 'dummy run' on Lady Louis to assess her reaction. Only instead of wearing his new suit, he put on his old tail coat and trousers. When his wife came into the bedroom he slyly asked, 'What do you think, Edwina?'

October 1946. Lady Patricia's wedding to Sir John Knatchbull, 7th Baron Brabourne. Back row, left to right: The Duchess of Kent, Lord Louis, H.M. King George VI, Lady Louis, the best man Squadron Leader Charles Harris-St.John. Middle row: Lady Brabourne, Lord Louis' mother the Dowager Marchioness of Milford Haven, the bridegroom, the bride, H.M the Queen, (unknown). Bridesmaids: Lady Pamela, Princess Alexandra of Kent, Princess Margaret, Princess Elizabeth

Above: On board the royal yacht *Victoria and Albert* during a Review of the Fleet

Left: As an R.A.F. sergeant at R.A.F. Mount Batten in Plymouth

She shook her head with disappointment.

'I can't see any difference from your old outfit,' she said.

Lord Louis smiled.

'Ah,' he exclaimed, 'you are right, Edwina. It's my old outfit. Now have a look at this.'

In an instant he changed and Lady Louis glowed with praise.

'Dickie, you look a different person,' she said, 'it's perfectly cut . . . absolutely first class.'

Lord Louis' pleasure brought Hawes and Curtis a bonus. His Lordship ordered six new suits and asked them to make his Naval uniforms too. They also became responsible for the livery of the household staff and Lord Louis gave me permission for my one personal suit a year, part of my allowance, to be made by the same tailors. Assuming that I was personally settling the bill, Hawes and Curtis only charged seven guineas, a gesture, I am sure, intended to reciprocate all the unexpected trade I had brought them!

Only Lord Louis could ask, 'How do you manage to get your suits for seven guineas when mine cost fifty? Have you got some special deal going, Charles?'

One of His Lordship's passions, no doubt due to the number of days he spent in uniform, was for hats. We were in Jamaica when I bought a Panama hat for 15 shillings (75p) after bartering with the shop-owner. Lord Louis had pushed aside the same hat because it was priced at £3. He settled for a much cheaper version.

When I got into the car wearing the Panama, His Lordship exclaimed, 'That's the one I wanted, Charles, but I couldn't afford it myself. Maybe I pay you too much if you can manage to buy hats like that.'

I said, 'But I only paid 15 shillings for it, m'Lord.'

'You couldn't have done,' His Lordship said tetchily, 'it was priced £3, I saw it on the label myself.'

'Yes, m'Lord, you did. But in a shop like that they expect a customer to barter over the price.'

Lord Louis sighed. 'Yes, maybe, Charles. But I couldn't haggle like that.'

'I understand, m'Lord,' I said, 'it's difficult when you've got a title. You can't do those kind of things.'

I took off my hat and admired it.

'I must say it is a very nice Panama, m'Lord,' I said, 'I'm very lucky to have got it at the price. It was a bargain.'

A few days later His Lordship had to attend a Naval review in Kingston harbour. He was to go in civilian clothes and he put on a very smart tropical suit. As he was getting dressed he despatched me to the kitchen to get a glass of orange juice for him, but when I returned His Lordship had disappeared. More mysteriously – so had my Panama hat!

This little subterfuge he attempted to repeat the following week when he was due to attend another civil function. This time I was quicker on my toes and I took him in my Panama hat as well as the orange drink before he could move.

Lord Louis was dumbfounded.

'Charles, you've rumbled me,' he said, bursting into laughter. 'You don't mind me wearing your hat?'

'Wear it whenever you wish, m'Lord,' I said. 'Besides, it suits you a lot better than it does me!'

The Panama hat had a long innings and when His Lordship was installed as Viceroy of India and he wanted to wear it once more, he said to me, 'Look, Charles, I must buy this hat from you. Charge what you feel it is worth and put it down on your expense sheet.'

Each week I kept a list of expenses paid out on Lord Louis' behalf – like the cost of hair lotion, shaving sticks and other toiletries – but I never did enter down the cost of the Panama. Somehow I considered it was a gift I really owed him.

There was a funny sequel. When we were in the Mediterranean, I accidentally crossed the quarter deck of one of Lord Louis' destroyers – apparently breaking an unwritten law. Even in civilian clothes one had to wear a hat before crossing such a hallowed deck!

'Charles! What are you doing?' thundered Lord Louis, positively fuming when he saw me. 'Don't you know you should not walk on to a quarter deck of one of His Majesty's ships without wearing a hat?'

'No, m'Lord, I didn't,' I said apologetically. 'I'm sorry, but I haven't got a hat to my name . . .'

And then I thought back.

'Mind,' I added, 'I used to own a Panama.'

5

Abdication

I was officially promoted to be Lord Louis' valet in 1936. a year that was surely to mark the most eventful days in my service.

King George V, who had celebrated his Silver Jubilee only seven months before, died on 20 January and the Royal family and the whole nation went into mourning. The only salvation from such gloom was the proclamation of the Prince of Wales as King. The Prince was a much adored figure, particularly among the working class, whose problems in the areas of housing and unemployment he had actively sought to resolve during the Depression.

Lord Louis was particularly happy on the declaration of the Prince of Wales as King Edward VIII. Not only were they cousins, they were the closest of friends. Indeed, the Prince of Wales had been Lord Louis' best man when he married. The remarkable thing was that the two men were so much alike, if not in looks, then in ways. The Prince of Wales possessed a friendly, genial manner; there wasn't a shred of pomposity in his nature and neither was Lord Louis affected by the mantle of rank. They both cared about the common cause.

There was every reason to believe that King Edward VIII would be a truly fine, crusading Sovereign, and I don't think any of us who were so closely involved inside the Royal corridors realized how the King's personal emotions were to divert the course of history. When he was the Prince of Wales we all knew that he enjoyed a busy social life and there was widespread speculation about who his bride would be.

When Mrs Wallis Simpson appeared in the Prince's life, I don't think many of his friends immediately suspected any danger until the friendship gained the momentum it did. Maybe I should have guessed more when Lord and Lady Louis joined the Prince of Wales and Mrs Simpson in Monte Carlo to enjoy a few days' relaxation, but there was still no real indication of what was to come.

I had first met Mrs Simpson at Balmoral on a weekend shoot. Every season it was customary to take part in the grouse and pheasant shooting parties, usually on one of the Royal estates. I was the keeper of Lord Louis' 12-bore shotgun and Her Ladyship's 16-bore gun, both of which had come from Purdey's. Normally I would act as loader, having taken instruction with Lord Louis at a shooting school on the Great West Road out of London.

At Balmoral that particular weekend the Prince of Wales was in characteristically high spirits, joking about the wretched weather and the lack of game but reserving a twinkle in his eye for Mrs Simpson, encouraging her to trail behind us in the shoot.

'You be careful where you point that gun, David,' she laughed, when he was grabbing her arm in a jocular fashion.

'Don't worry, Wallis,' he said, 'it's not loaded.'

Mrs Simpson dressed smartly for the shoot. She had changed into a warm tweed costume and boots. I found her very friendly and considerate, far from the dominating type of woman the public was led to believe she was.

'I imagine we are going to have pheasant for dinner tonight, Charles?' she said, her American accent not nearly so pronounced as I imagined it would be. She laughed, 'That's if they manage to shoot any!'

The Prince caught her remark.

'Do you hear what Wallis is saying, Dickie?' he exclaimed, turning to Lord Louis with a wide grin on his face. 'I think Wallis has thrown down a challenge.'

It was a wonderful, carefree day and those of us who were merely followers were made to feel part of the expedition. As it happened it was a reasonably good day's bag and, sure enough, pheasant was on that night's dinner menu, although I am sure a brace or two had already been put by in the kitchens for the occasion. Nevertheless, the Prince joked with Mrs Simpson over dinner about her remarks.

'Who said we weren't good enough?' he teased.

In the coming months he saw more and more of Mrs Simpson and it was very clear that he had fallen in love with her. Whenever he came to the house, or Lord Louis visited him, Mrs Simpson was invariably present. She and her second husband, Ernest Simpson, an American businessman, were apparently in the throes of divorce. There was growing conjecture on what would happen to the monarchy, and the clouds darkened for His Majesty when he decided to marry Mrs Simpson after her divorce came through in the autumn.

It was then that the world learned of the crisis, as a divorced woman could not be crowned Queen or even marry in the Church of England. Prime Minister Baldwin went to see the King at Fort Belvedere and so did Lord Louis, whose concern was evident to us all. I think Lord Louis did his best to persuade the King not to abdicate, because I heard him repeat, 'He can't do it. He mustn't do it!'

On the night before the King took his fateful decision, Lord Louis called me and asked me to drive him with all urgency to Fort Belvedere in Sunningdale. When we got there it was to discover that the King had not only summoned Lord Louis, but his three brothers as well.

It was obviously very crucial and as I waited for His Lordship in the stewards' room situated at the rear of the house, where the King's own maids and butlers were morosely gathered, the significance of the meeting did not escape any of us.

One of the servants poured tea, but it did not put much cheer into our spirits. In our hearts we knew the conclusion.

When the pantry bell rang, reassembling the staff, I walked round to the drive with the chauffeurs of the Royal dukes. Lord Louis wasn't too long in emerging. His face was ashen and his lips taut. Silently, he got into the car and we returned to London without conversation. There was no reason for Lord Louis to convey the news to me. His face did it all.

The next day, 10 December 1936, King Edward made his abdication broadcast, which left the country in a state of bewilderment and shock.

Upon Lord Louis fell a heavy burden, to console and comfort the ex-King on the one hand, while at the same time offering advice and support to Prince Albert, the Duke of York, who was now to take his brother's place on the throne as King George VI.

The former Prince of Wales and his bride, who were to become the Duke and Duchess of Windsor, departed into an almost reclusive extistence. Ironically, one of Lord Louis' first missions commanding H.M.S. *Kelly* was to go to Cherbourg to collect the Duke and Duchess and take them to Britain, ensuring their safety in the threatening war with Germany. The lifelong friendship between Lord Louis and his cousin was never affected by these dramatic events.

In the meantime, the nation warmed to King George VI after his Coronation. One might have regarded His Majesty as being a rather remote figure, but his reticent nature was seen to be due to his extreme shyness. Sometimes in conversation he stammered, but he overcame this affliction in time and in the years ahead he was able to win the admiration and respect of the people.

I got to like His Majesty as much as his brother. They were very different men, the new King being much less of an extrovert, but there were qualities that they both possessed. Not least, sensitivity and kindness. King George also had a keen sense of humour as was shown on a pheasant shoot at Sandringham to which Lord Louis was invited.

His Majesty, reversing accepted procedures, sent a page boy to my room, with an unexpected request.

'Mr Smith,' said the page boy, 'the King's Land Rover will be at the front door at 9.15 a.m. and His Majesty would take great pleasure if you would join him in the shoot.'

I think Lord Louis became a little jealous, especially when the King invited me to share a bowl of soup with him, poured from two hot flasks he produced from the deep pockets of his hacking jacket.

Lord Louis raised his eyebrows and said, 'Why you, Charles, and not me? Am I being left out of things?'

The King was equally hospitable when I accompanied Lord Louis aboard the Royal yacht, the *Victoria and Albert*, for the review of the Naval fleet assembled off Weymouth. The yacht was nothing less than a floating palace, with the walls of cabins and salons covered from floor to ceiling in silk tapestry, the gangways laid with thickly piled red carpets, and pillars artistically disguised as sycamore trees.

Perhaps His Majesty was too hospitable, because for the first time in my life I became intoxicated. The Royal barge ran a shuttle service for a series of cocktail parties that were being hosted on the decks of some of the parading vessels.

'What's stopping you, Charles?' His Majesty said persuasively. 'Lord Louis won't mind if you go off and have a good time.'

I took His Majesty at his word, and the Navy entertained Lord Mountbatten's valet in a style to which he was unaccustomed.

It was in the early hours that I crawled back on board the *Victoria and Albert* and all I remember thinking, through my throbbing head, was that I had to arouse Lord Louis at 7.00 a.m. Somehow I kept awake, suffering the cruellest of hangovers.

Lord Louis eyed my red, blotchy face, but didn't say anything as I got him into his ceremonial robes for the Review. He was to wear a frock coat and leather half-Wellingtons polished to the brilliance of patent leather. When finally I clipped on the belt for his holster and sword, he gave a nod of approval in the mirror and remarked, 'Well, Charles, I don't know how you managed it but everything looks fine. That must have taken some perseverance, as I hear you had a bit of a bender last night. Am I right?'

I groaned my reply through a thick melancholy haze.

His Lordship was sympathetic.

'Most of us have one drink too many at some stage in our lives,' he said, 'and I'm sure you won't feel like allowing it to happen again. I think the best thing you can do to shake off the hangover is to go and get a good sleep. We're not leaving until three o'clock and I shan't want you until then.'

Mumbling my gratitude, I meekly went off to my bunk where I slept through the main part of the Review. On the Royal train back to London, I kept a low profile, declining any further drink that was offered to me!

There were one or two other occasions when Lord Louis might have had cause to despair of me. I once danced the night away with an American millionairess in Miami who asked Lord Louis, 'You don't mind, Dickie, if I borrow your valet, now do you?'

When I reported for duty the next morning, His Lordship noticed I was still wearing my evening dress trousers. I had not found time to change out of them.

'Good heavens, Charles, the way you're carrying on you'll be in the gossip columns if you're not careful,' quipped His Lordship.

Feeling exhausted I crept into a bunk at the rear of the fuselage in the twin-engined seaplane that was to take us on to Jamaica that day. I thought I would have a quiet forty winks, but Lord Louis, discovering that I had not occupied my seat, was convinced I had not boarded the plane and instructed the pilot to return to Miami to collect me! Luckily, a member of the crew found me curled up in the rear bunk before the plane had altered course.

With exasperation ringing in his voice, Lord Louis told me, 'The next time we're in Miami, please remind me not to let you go dancing!'

My high jinks in Germany landed me in more trouble. When His Lordship was staying at Darmstadt Palace as a guest of his uncle, the Grand Duke Ernest Louis of Hesse, I ventured out for a night on the tiles. I had been invited to a beer garden party and when I got back to the Palace at 1.00 a.m. it was locked, and despite incessant ringing of the night bell I could not arouse anyone. Then I spotted a magnolia tree close to the open window of my bedroom in the Palace. I clambered up the branches only to be hauled down by my ankles by the Palace guards, who suddenly appeared from out of the darkness.

The guards didn't speak English and I could not communicate with them in German, so I was arrested and unceremoniously bundled into a cell of the Guard House. However, as I kept mentioning Lord Mountbatten's name, the officer-in-charge sought a translator who eventually appeared in his pyjamas and dressing gown and was able to establish that I wasn't an intruder but a valet with my own room in the Palace itself.

Profuse apologies followed and at 7.30 a.m. I was released, but my position was still quite ominous. I did not relish the prospect of arousing Lord Louis thirty minutes later than scheduled. It might have been safer to have stayed in the cell! I should not have worried.

Over breakfast Lord Louis was treated to the tale of my adventures and at a Palace banquet that night he summoned me before the tables and announced, 'Here is our prisoner . . .' to the delight of all the guests. I stood shame-faced muttering my regrets and I am sure Lord Louis savoured every moment of my discomfort!

Unfortunately, the happiness of this period abruptly ended. The Grand Duke died shortly afterwards and then came a tragedy of enormous proportions when five other members of the Grand Duke's family were killed when their plane crashed in fog at Ostend on their way to London for the wedding of his son Louis, the Prince of Hesse and the Rhine, to the Honourable Margaret Geddes.

Then Lord Louis suffered another bitter blow. His elder brother Georgie, the second Marquess of Milford Haven, died of cancer. He was only forty-six. Lord Louis held his brother in the highest regard and said of him, 'He must have been one of the cleverest men I have ever known. I think his brain was twice the size of mine. Everybody loved him. I don't think he had an enemy in the world.

More sad news was still to come. Lady Louis' father, Lord Mount Temple, died and again the household was plunged into mourning.

This series of tragedies, which occurred in the span of two years, weighed greatly upon Lord Louis as well as his wife. But his one cure, as always in adversity, was to immerse himself more determinedly into his work. And with the outbreak of the Second World War upon us, there was no time to look back or linger on heartbreak.

6

War

Ten days before the Second World War broke out, Lord Louis took command of H.M.S. *Kelly* – a moment he treasured almost as much as the birth of his two daughters. For His Lordship had witnessed the *Kelly*'s 'birth' from the very moment its keel was laid at the Hebburn-on-Tyne shipbuilder's yard. Every weekend we had gone to Newcastle to watch the destroyer's progress.

Various managers and foremen of the company would anticipate His Lordship's arrival, but they had to wait their turn. Lord Louis would impatiently intercept the first worker he saw on the site to enquire, 'How far have we got this week?' while eyeing the ship's growing hull to make his own on-the-spot assessment.

We travelled to Newcastle by train, leaving the Rolls behind. But in time Lord Louis bought a little Austin Seven so that we got round the city as well as make the run to the shipbuilder's yard. I would perform the duties of chauffeur, opening and closing the door for His Lordship, whose mind was so wrapped up with the project that he didn't seem to notice any difference between the use of the Austin and the Rolls.

When finally the *Kelly* was launched, His Lordship was as ecstatic as a schoolboy with a new toy, and the destroyer set sail for Chatham to undertake its trials. I spent a week aboard with His Lordship during this operation and I became convinced, once and for all, that I would never make a sailor!

As war broke out, I summoned courage to tell His Lordship. 'I am sorry, m'Lord, and this is nothing personal, but I don't think I am qualified for the Navy. I'm going to volunteer for the R.A.F.'

His Lordship held me squarely in the eye.

'Charles, you could not have made a better decision,' he said. 'I don't want to injure your feelings, but I don't honestly think you've got the legs – or the stomach – for the sea.'

When friends asked why I was ignoring the Navy, I would joke with them, 'You can't have two Admirals in one house, can you?' a remark which brought a twinkle to Lord Louis' eyes.

I tried to enlist with the R.A.F. that week. By coincidence my brother Jim served at R.A.F. Mount Batten, a flying boat station off Plymouth Sound that bore a truncated version of His Lordship's title, although as far as I knew there was no connection. It was there I first ventured to begin my military career, but I was told that I would have to await my official call-up papers. Nevertheless, I was made a civilian steward of the Officers' Mess, a post I continued to occupy with the rank of Sergeant when my papers came through after completing six weeks' 'square bashing' at a station near Blackpool.

Lord Louis visited R.A.F. Mount Batten on three occasions while I served there and he was presented with the Station's crest inscribed 'In Honour Bound' and mounted on a plaque. Later he gave me the plaque as a present and said, 'I feel that you are more entitled to it than I am.'

When he made his first visit to the Mount Batten base I was still in civilian clothes and he joked with me, 'Haven't they got you into uniform yet, Charles?' Until that point no one on the base knew that I had been his valet and the Commanding Officer, a Group Captain, was enraged.

'Why didn't you tell us?' he blared, rapping his desk with his cane while I stood wondering what difference it would have made. I didn't like to curry favour by indiscriminately using His Lordship's name. I wasn't in the habit of name-dropping and there were a lot of names that I could have tumbled out had I wanted to impress anyone at that period. But it agitated the C.O., who was just as surprised when I came to be recognized by the Duke of Kent, then a ferry pilot, who made a special request to see me on his visit to the Station.

I was seconded to look after the Duke, who was staying only for one night, and at dawn the following morning I was up to organize his departure for Scotland. In the bay were dotted several Sunderlands and other flying boats. The Duke was journeying in a Catalina which was already turning over its engines, ready for his embarkation.

'Goodbye, Charles,' said the Duke, in flying helmet and jacket, as he stepped on to the barge to take him out to the plane, 'I'll tell Lord Louis I've seen you here.'

The weather was fine and it looked like being a nice day; I saw the Duke safely board the Catalina from the barge. Then I heard the roar of the engines as they were put into full throttle and the Catalina hurtled through the sea in a cloud of spray. I watched until the plane was just a speck in the sky and then I walked back to the Mess.

It was the Duke of Kent's last journey. The seaplane crashed into the mountains, well off course, and no one could explain why it had been in that position.

Shock and sadness filled me. I could still see the Duke as he was that morning, his cheeks rosy from the wind that whipped in from the sea. A fine life had been lost – and the lives too of his valet and the aircraft crew. None had survived. I felt greatly for the Duchess and their three young children; how would they take such a terrible blow? I went back to my duties heavy in heart.

Lord Louis and the *Kelly* were by now in the thick of the war. She was damaged by a mine when searching for U-boats off the Tyne, and in the Norwegian campaign she was badly torpedoed but Lord Louis defied an Admiral's order to scuttle his ship. Eventually she was towed back to the Tyne by a rescuing tug, despite being attacked by an E-boat and the Luftwaffe.

After the *Kelly* was recommissioned she was sent into action in the Mediterranean. During the Battle of Crete, in which she played a vital role, she was attacked by twenty-four Junkers 87 dive-bombers and she sank – with Lord Louis still on the bridge. He swam to a life raft, the sea swirling around him. He was saved along with a handful of other oil-smeared survivors who were machine-gunned in the water. More than half of the *Kelly*'s officers and men were lost.

Lord Louis never forgot that experience. He talked of it often in later years and he told me, 'It was one of the real moments in my life when I was frightened, Charles. We were just sitting targets and there was nothing we could do. We were helpless.'

His Lordship's epitaph for the *Kelly* was typical. 'We swore we would never leave her,' he said, 'and we didn't. She left us!'

In later times, a *Kelly* Reunion Association was formed by the surviving members of the lower deck. There was not a ship that sailed throughout the war that had been served by a more faithful or loving crew. No wonder Noël Coward was moved to immortalize their exploits in his subsequent film.

Alas, my own career in the R.A.F. saw very little action and I became impatient to become involved in a more positive way than by just remaining an Officers' Mess steward. I applied for a transfer and was fortunate enough to get one. This led to a series of postings which took me to a station on the south coast and another in Ireland before being sent overseas to India. This, I thought, was more like it, but the war had passed by the camp at Secunderabad, much to my frustration. I wrote a letter to Lord Louis, who was then Supreme Allied Commander. His forces had practically run the Japanese out of Burma. Lord Louis had kept in touch with me and he always said, 'If you ever come out East, then please let me know, Charles.'

I posted my letter at the camp's mail box at 4.00 p.m. Two hours later a couple of Sergeants arrived at my billet and one of them told me, 'I'm sorry, Sergeant Smith, but we've been ordered to put you under open arrest. You're to come and see the Commanding Officer.'

'For what offence?' I asked, totally perplexed.

'I'm sorry, Sergeant. We don't know. We've just been ordered to bring you in by the C.O.'

I straightened my uniform and got my cap. I marched with them to the station headquarters. The C.O. was waiting for me.

'Is this your letter, Sergeant?' he asked.

'Yes, Sir, it is,' I said.

'Didn't you know, Sergeant, that it is an offence to write to the Supreme Allied Commander or any other commander without the consent of your own station chief?'

I nodded my head. 'But I am not writing to Lord Mountbatten about a military matter or airing any kind of grievance,' I said.

The C.O. was troubled.

'Then what reason could you possibly have for writing to the Supreme Allied Commander?' he asked.

'Well, Sir, it is a private matter and I would rather not go into detail. But in civilian life I am Lord Mountbatten's valet.'

'Are you indeed? Well, I suppose that throws a different light on the matter,' said the C.O., his frown clearing.

He still harboured some suspicion, however, for he made me sign a form confirming that the letter was written by me and that it did not contain a grievance.

Lord Louis replied within a fortnight, but his letter was intercepted as mine had been and it was confiscated by the C.O., who sent for my presence once more.

'It seems you have a reply, Sergeant,' said the C.O., handing me the letter, his voice carrying sufficient curiosity for me to know that he required me to open it in front of him.

Quickly, I sped through the contents and gave it to the C.O. to read. It was a typically chatty letter from Lord Louis, telling of a week's leave he had spent in England, but my eye had been caught by the postscript which read, 'I may want to borrow you to open up Government House Singapore for me.'

My Commanding Officer was notably impressed and at that very moment his telephone rang. He picked up the receiver and said, 'Yes, who's there?'

Slowly his face changed expression as he talked, and he looked at me as though I was the subject of the conversation. When he put down the receiver, a sigh escaped his lips.

'That is quite extraordinary, Sergeant,' he said. 'Do you gather what that was all about?'

'No, Sir,' I said.

'It was a message from Divisional Headquarters. The Supreme Allied Commander has already sent for you and you must leave for

SOUTH EAST ASIA COMMAND HEADQUARTERS.

21st August 1945

My dear Charles

Thank you for your letter of the 25th July, which I found
here on my return from Europe where I had been to attend conferences in Berlin and London. I had my first week's leave at
Broadlands since 1941, and enjoyed it very much. You will be
sorry to hear that Mrs. Lankester has died and so has the cook
at 15 Chester St., Mrs. D'Arcey (though you may not have known
her). The staff at Broadlands now consists of the butler, Frank
Randall (who was a sergeant in the Home Guard), and Lord Mount
Temple's retired valet, Aldridge, who helps part time. There
is no chauffeur, except the electrician Sullivan, and no housekeeper or housemaid, except for a charwoman. The chef, Brinz,
is still going strong. Jessie, the Head Housemaid, is at
Chester St. with our old butler and valet-chauffeur, Emsley,
and they run this little house between them.

Of course I remember seeing you at the Mountbatten Air
Station, and was glad to find you had got on so well in the Air
Force. Heath joined the Fleet Air Arm and ▮▮▮▮▮▮ the Navy
(Combined Ops.)

I visited the S. of T.T. Hakimpet about a year ago, but
of course you were not out there then. If I come your way
again I shall make a point of looking you up.

I expect that it will take me anything up to 9 months to
clear up the mess the Japanese have made in the Far East.

Yours sincerely

Louis Mountbatten

P. S. I may want to borrow you to open up
government House Singapore for me.

Kandy in Ceylon immediately. You had better get back to your billet and get your things packed. I will arrange for your flight now.'

I thanked him, saluted, and made my exit.

Early the next morning the C.O. sent his own staff car to take me out to the waiting Dakota on the airstrip, where an officer was asked to relinquish his seat so that it could be allocated to me as my mission was deemed more 'urgent'.

After two re-fuelling stops and an overnight halt in Colombo, I finally arrived in Kandy where I was soon to find headquarters. My papers were barely checked before I was conducted to the offices of the Supreme Allied Commander.

Lord Louis looked well and sun-bronzed, cutting an elegant, aristocratic figure in his khaki drill uniform. As we were meeting under military terms, I stood to attention and saluted. I thought I detected a wry smile curl His Lordship's lips. I may have been a Sergeant, but in his mind I was still his valet!

'Charles, how good to see you,' he said, shaking my hand, 'but what kept you? According to my mathematics you should have been here last night.'

I explained that we hade made an overnight stop en route and he shrugged acceptance. He motioned for me to take a chair and to relax.

'I will show you to your room in a minute,' he said. 'I have approved it myself. You will find it is very comfortable. First, let me hear what you've been doing during the war, Charles. I want to hear all about it.'

I felt suddenly embarrassed. My experiences were so insignificant compared to His Lordship's. His name was hallowed throughout South-East Asia, a man whose courage and leadership had brought him Burma's most coveted honours and decorations. Unconsciously, my stare caught Lord Louis' fresh chest ribbons and I tried to identify them. His Lordship must have guessed what I was thinking, because he rose from his desk and picked up a green leather-faced wooden box that I instantly recognized. It was Lord Louis' decoration box, one that I had bought in London at Spink's for £6 just before the outbreak of war.

As His Lordship brought the box over from the other side of the

A Souvenir of India – 1947

Mountbatten of Burma   *Edwina Mountbatten of Burma*   *Kinsey*

and Lady Louis, Viceroy and Vicereine of India, in the throne room of Government House, Delhi

Gandhi and Lord Louis taking tea on the lawn at Government House in Delhi. Gandhi declined the scones and sandwiches and ate a bowl of goat's curd instead

Lord Louis' York MW102

room and placed it on the desk, I began to feel slightly uneasy. For when I originally purchased it Lord Louis had given me a terrible rollicking.

'It's far too big, Charles,' he said, 'you're a bloody fool. No one could win enough decorations to fill this box. I've a good mind to make you pay for the bloody thing.'

Now, as he unlocked the box all these years later, I was preparing myself for another castigation. 'Surely,' I thought to myself, 'he is not going to have another go at me for buying that damn box.'

But no, His Lordship smiled at me and reflected, 'Charles, do you remember when I tore you up a strip for buying this box to put my medals in? I thought it was too massive at the time and I think I told you so.'

I nodded, 'Yes, m'Lord. You did just that.'

'Well, Charles,' His Lordship continued, 'I take back everything I said. Just have a peep at it. There isn't room to put another medal or ribbon in.'

I picked up some of the colours and examined them, airing at the same time my own dissatisfaction at having played such a futile role during the war.

'Ah,' said Lord Louis, 'you've caught up with the action at last, Charles. But you are only just in time. I believe the Japanese are on the verge of surrender.'

There was an absolute finality to Lord Louis' words, and with good reason. Briefed by Winston Churchill and President Truman, Lord Louis was privy to the top-secret American plan to drop the war's first atomic bombs on Hiroshima and Nagasaki.

Lord Louis was right. The Japanese surrender was upon us, but in order not to arouse suspicion, Lord Louis gave the go-ahead for 'Operation Zipper' in the re-conquest of Malaya.

That short spell at Kandy was hectic while preparations were made for our move to Singapore, and I must confess I saw little of Lord Louis, until on 5 September 1945 I flew with him and General Sir William Slim into Singapore, which the Allied Forces now occupied. We flew in Lord Louis' special York MW102 plane – one that was put at his personal disposal all through the war and was now to serve him in times of peace. We were given a fighter escort for the journey and a transport plane followed, carrying Lord Louis' equipment and jeeps.

As the York circled over Singapore, we could see our troops taking command from the surrendering Japanese who were laying down their arms. It was a proud moment for Lord Louis and he turned to one of his senior staff and said, 'Thank God it is all over.'

We disembarked and made our way to Government House, which had been left in reasonably good order by the Japanese. It was an impressive white building and now the Union Jack was flying from its parapets. Lord Louis put me in charge of allocating the available accommodation to the officers and men who were to be billeted in the huge building. It was quite a task, but made easier by the help of those civilians who poured back into the city once they were assured the Japanese had gone. Curtains, carpets and furnishings had to be found, but bedding was the main priority, and as if this wasn't enough, I was asked to prepare a special dinner, a Victory Banquet.

It was all very well, as I told Lord Louis, but a banquet wouldn't go very far on four tins of dehydrated potatoes and a couple of canisters of chopped luncheon meat! Those were the only stocks left in the kitchen.

Again, I was rescued by our local friends who took me out to stores in the city in a Queen Mary truck. Soon, and to my amazement, it was crammed full with supplies of fish, chicken, ham, potatoes and vegetables. We also obtained a harvest of melons!

An exclusive regiment of generals, admirals and air marshals flew into Singapore for the celebrations, and never was there a happier host than Lord Louis. Especially when he saw the banquet I had prepared.

'It's reassuring to know that you can perform miracles, Charles,' he smiled.

Seven days later the formal surrender ceremony was arranged in the Council Chamber of Singapore Town Hall where Lord Louis, flanked by his senior officers, accepted the surrender of 680,879 Japanese in South-East Asia in the presence of military representatives of the United States, India, Australia, China, France and Holland. Lord Louis demanded that the Japanese supreme commanders should not only sign the surrender treaty, but hand over their ceremonial swords, thus stripping them of their last vestments of honour and dignity. I was able to watch the ceremony.

Throughout the whole of South-East Asia the concentration camps run by the Japanese were to reveal a horrifying picture. Our captured men had suffered the most terrible atrocities. Many were close to death from their tortures, if not from starvation.

Lady Louis, who was Superintendent-in-Chief of the St John Ambulance Brigade and Chairman of its Joint War Organization with the Red Cross, flew in to conduct 'Operation Mercy'. She covered 76,000 miles visiting the prisoner of war camps and hospitals, medical centres, and convalescent depots. Her Ladyship tended the sick and the dying, as well as giving fresh hope to the living. In the eyes of thousands she was as much a heroine as Florence Nightingale had been.

My problems in Singapore were quite domestic, but starvation was still apparent. The staple diet of the local Chinese, on whose work force I relied to keep the camp running, was rice. We had none, but I raided a cargo ship just in from Thailand being unloaded at the dockhead and managed to get a dozen bags, which were loaded on to my jeep by a group of Japanese prisoners of war. Back at the base the Chinese workers greeted me like a hero!

I stayed in Singapore for nearly ten months assisting Lord Louis, whose task seemed beyond normal human endurance. Liberation wasn't the end of the story; the needs of 128 million people were now his responsibility. Food supplies had to be found, communications established, and civilian police forces drafted. These were the essentials, but there were thousands of other problems.

In those circumstances I didn't feel it was the proper time to worry Lord Louis with my own troubles, which burst upon me in a letter from London. I couldn't fool His Lordship for long, however; he had a unique knack of detecting when something was wrong.

'Well, Charles, what is it?' he asked one morning after returning from his regular ride before breakfast. 'It's no good keeping it to yourself any longer, Charles. For God's sake, I know when you're off colour . . .'

'I didn't tell you because you've got too many other important things to think about, m'Lord,' I said, 'but I've heard from London that I've been cited in a divorce case!'

For a moment Lord Louis appeared rather stunned. I don't think he had ever considered that his valet, whose conduct he required to be exemplary, might become involved in a scandal of that nature.

'I think you had better come up to my office, Charles, and I will see if there is any way I can help you,' he said.

All through the war I had kept one secret from Lord and Lady Louis – that I was in love with a W.A.A.F. whose first marriage had floundered. For a spell she had lived with me in the married quarters of one of the R.A.F. stations I served on. No one suspected that we were not legally married because I was able to tell everyone in absolute honesty, 'This is Mrs Smith.'

My W.A.A.F. was named Violet Smith – heaven knows why she should contemplate marriage to another Smith, but she did! This minor deception suited us perfectly. Even the local butcher and grocer assumed we were nothing other than a legitimately married couple, after all 'Mr Charles Smith' and 'Mrs Violet Smith' were clearly stamped on our ration books! Obviously, we didn't give anyone reason to suspect that we weren't really married. We wanted to marry legally, but the war divided us and Violet's divorce took so long in coming through.

Once over the initial shock of being cited as a co-respondent, my feelings turned to joy because it now meant that Violet was free. I told Lord Louis, 'We want to marry very much and as I am due to be demobbed, I wonder if I can ask you for an early release, m'Lord?'

Lord Louis stroked his chin thoughtfully as he listened to my story.

'Let me see what I can do, Charles,' he said, still smarting over my reluctance at not having mentioned the matter before.

Lady Louis caught a snatch of our conversation and was intrigued by it all.

'How did you manage to keep it such a secret, Charles?' she asked. 'It must have been a shade embarrassing, or did you use false names?'

Her Ladyship had not gathered that Violet's surname was the same as mine and when I repeated this to her, she remarked,

'Charles, you always were lucky, weren't you! It is one of the most romantic stories I have ever heard.'

Lord Louis mellowed and in his office the next morning he gave me two personally signed letters that he hoped would expedite my passage home to England.

'It's impossible to guarantee you a seat on a plane out, Charles, I'm afraid,' he said. 'Every plane is packed tight, but you might hitch your way out on one of the cargo planes. These two letters will help you on your way.'

As I turned to leave his office, His Lordship said, 'And Charles – good luck! I will see you back in England – in civilian life I hope!'

I hitched a lift in an old Halifax that was delivering mail. I got to Calcutta and then to Bombay, where I had to stay for two nights awaiting further transport. Many of the N.C.O.'s recognized me from an earlier base and they welcomed me as the 'Supremo II'!

'Next to Lord Mountbatten, Charles is the most powerful man in South-East Asian command!' joked one N.C.O.

There were many men, and officers among them, listed for the draft home.

'Watch Charles and see how he'll pull a few strings,' an old Sergeant friend of mine winked. 'He'll get the V.I.P. treatment!'

I did too – thanks to Lord Louis' letters!

A passage was found for me on the French liner the *Louis Pasteur*, a ship that had been built for Blue Ribbon competition across the Atlantic but was requisitioned as a troop-carrier during the war. She was sailing for Southampton, her decks heaving with thousands of joyous troops on their way home.

I will never forget the morning when we sailed into the English Channel and the mist cleared to reveal the white cliffs of Dover. A tumultuous cry resounded from the decks; some of the men had not seen England or their loved ones since the start of the war. We were home at last!

I married Violet within two weeks of my demob from the R.A.F. We were married in the village of Worksop, near Doncaster, where my parents lived and where we were to establish residency. It was 8 January 1946.

By her previous marriage Violet had a daughter, Shirley, who called me 'Pip' – my mother's maiden name was Paxton (perhaps after the apple!) and Shirley's children were also to grow up calling me by the same name. They still do today!

Our marriage has been a very happy one; how much that has been due to Lord and Lady Louis you will come to gather in the following pages.

7

To India with the Viceroy

Lady Louis had inherited Broadlands on the death of her father, Lord Mount Temple, in 1939.

This beautiful Palladian-style mansion, situated at Romsey in Hampshire amid sweeping countryside, its lawns running down to the River Test, had been in the ownership of Her Ladyship's family and ancestors for more than 200 years, though the history of the house dated back still further, touching the fourteenth century.

Our move to Broadlands was unfortunately delayed by the outbreak of the Second World War. Very little could be moved from Adsdean at that time, and those belongings I was able to pack had to remain in storage.

The house was requisitioned and throughout the war it served as an annexe to the Royal South Hants Hospital, but when peacetime came Broadlands at last became the official and permanent home of Lord and Lady Louis on their return from Singapore.

I had only had one rushed glimpse of the house in 1939, but in the coming years was to come to know almost every square inch of Broadlands and its vast estate.

My first task there was to unpack the chests and trunks we had left behind at the beginning of the war. Amid the clothing I found one or two of my own suits, still in fine condition, that I had put away with Lord Louis'!

In the months I had been back in England awaiting His Lordship's return, I had settled into civilian life, taking a temporary post helping with the administrative processing necessary to enable G.I. brides to leave for America with their new husbands. But in the summer Lord and Lady Louis were back and kindly offered fresh employment, not only to me, but to Violet as well.

'You mustn't leave your wife behind,' insisted Lord Louis, 'and now that you *are* married you can live at Lee Lodge.'

His Lordship was a moralist – I am sure he would not have approved of me living in sin! In his eyes, one had to do the right and proper thing; conventional standards should not waiver.

Lee Lodge was on the south side of the estate and it was perfect for us, except that we really didn't have enough furniture to make a home. We bought the bare essentials – a bed, a kitchen table and two chairs – and I remember we were just getting things straight when a jeep pulled up outside the door and Lord Louis and Prince Philip climbed out.

Lord Louis smiled at the door. 'Charles, I think you know my nephew . . .' It wasn't difficult to recognize Prince Philip, even though he had grown into manhood. That winning glint in the eye was still there!

His Lordship wanted to see all over the house and Prince Philip followed on his heel. In our upstairs room they were intrigued by the sight of a chamber pot which Violet had left lying on top of the eiderdown.

'Do you always keep it there, Charles?' chuckled Prince Philip as I flushed with embarrassment.

We were happy at Lee Lodge and Violet came to work with me in the big house when things began to get busy, assisting with all the kitchen chores whenever Lord and Lady Louis were entertaining.

The routine at Broadlands fell very much into the familiar pre-war pattern of Adsdean, guests descending on us at weekends. The King and Queen would arrive with the Royal children, only they were no longer children. Princess Elizabeth was a mature and serene twenty-year-old, and Princess Margaret at sixteen was full of teen-age spirit. I felt honoured that they should remember me.

'You were in the R.A.F.? What did His Lordship think about that?' said Princess Elizabeth, interested to learn that I had not pursued Lord Louis' footsteps into the Royal Navy.

For Princess Margaret, my presence stirred childhood memories of Bozo the bush baby, and the mischief he caused.

'He was great fun, Charles, wasn't he?' said the Princess. 'Sometimes he was almost human. We did miss him when he died.'

The two Princesses were to figure in a very happy event in the Mountbatten household in October 1946, when Lady Patricia married Lord Brabourne, her father's wartime A.D.C. Princess Elizabeth and Princess Margaret were bridesmaids and their parents, the King and Queen, also attended the wedding at Romsey Abbey, the wedding procession passing through streets jostling with thousands of cheering well-wishers.

Lady Patricia was twenty-two years old and my thoughts were transported back to the day I had joined Lord and Lady Louis when she was just about to start school. She was so much like her father, not only in ways but in looks too, with high cheekbones and strong, distinguishing features. During the war she had served as a Wren officer.

She was radiant as a bride. Lord Louis was a very proud father, and a somewhat nervous one too, as I discovered while helping him to get ready for the wedding.

'Damn it, Charles, I wish you were giving the bride away,' he growled. 'I'm feeling more nervous than at any time throughout the whole war!'

I believed him.

By the time Lord Louis got to the foot of the staircase his Naval uniform was in disarray. Some of the tassels were twisted and King George alerted me before His Lordship could step outside the door.

'Something is wrong with Lord Louis' uniform, Charles,' he said. 'I think you had better put it right for him.'

'Yes, of course, Your Majesty,' I said, moving forward to adjust the tassels, 'but if only His Lordship wasn't so flustered the uniform would hang properly as it did when I dressed him upstairs.'

BROADLANDS,

ROMSEY,

HAMPSHIRE.

29th October, 1946.

My dear Charles,

      My wife and I will always be so
grateful to you for the help and co-operation
you have given over our daughter's wedding
arrangements.

      Everything was perfect and we
realise how much this was due to the work you
have done during these past weeks.

Yours truly

Mountbatten of Burma

His Majesty chuckled.

'I don't think I've ever seen Lord Louis in a state like this before,' he said.

Lady Patricia, by comparison, was calm and collected. Her father finally drew strength from her and his nervousness subsided once the ceremony began.

His Lordship was pleased with the match; Lord Brabourne had served with him through the turbulent days in Burma. He was the son of a former Governor of Bombay and Bengal and his father had also acted as temporary Viceroy of India for a six-month spell in 1938. All of this, of course, was coincidental to the events that were to overtake Lord Louis in the early part of 1947, but I am sure that Lord Brabourne must have pondered on the fact that the role once played by his father was taken by his father-in-law.

We had now moved the London residence from Brook House to one in Chester Street. It was a far more compact house and suited Lord and Lady Louis' purposes perfectly when they were in town.

On New Year's Day a call came from No. 10 Downing Street: Prime Minister Clement Attlee wanted to see Lord Louis urgently. His Lordship didn't have an inkling as to why the Prime Minister wanted to see him and as I was hurrying him along that morning he said, 'Heaven knows what he wants, Charles, but I imagine it must be something important. How often does one get called to No. 10 Downing Street?'

When Lord Louis came home, looking apprehensive and somewhat distant in expression, my curiosity grew. I guessed that something was afoot on a high level; there was a sudden flurry of activity. His secretarial staff and his newly appointed A.D.C., Lieutenant-Commander Peter Howes, were summoned by His Lordship. A day or two later His Lordship confided in me and by then I am sure that official word had been transmitted in Whitehall, if it hadn't yet been leaked to the press.

Mr Attlee had appointed Lord Louis Viceroy of India, replacing Lord Wavell in Delhi. His Lordship had already been created an Earl and had taken the title of 'Mountbatten of Burma'. His special mission in India was to see the country through to its promised independence.

Time became of the utmost priority.

'I'm afraid I am going to have to get a complete new wardrobe, Charles,' said Lord Louis. 'Can you arrange it for me?'

I made out a list of necessary tropical clothing and white colonial-style uniforms that His Lordship was likely to need and I took it along to Hawes and Curtis.

Lady Louis also had a lot of packing she wanted my assistance with. She felt it was necessary, not knowing what crockery and domestic utensils might exist in Delhi's Government House where we would be residing, to take out a good reserve stock of our Broadlands linen, cutlery and dinner plates, all of which had to be meticulously wrapped. Lady Louis' jewellery casket also had to be stowed for the journey, the collection included the diamond tiara that she would wear as Vicereine at the proclamation ceremony.

The tiara was a gift from Lord Louis and he had personally designed it. It was unique. Mounted on platinum, the tiara could be taken apart to form a necklace, braclet, brooch and ear rings.

When His Lordship gave it to his wife, he said, 'Darling, I am giving you four presents in one.'

'Four presents?' questioned Lady Louis.

'Yes,' chuckled her husband, showing how the tiara could be broken down. 'Isn't this better? How often do you wear a tiara? Now you will be able to make regular use of it and who will know?

As a Viscount and Viceroy, the Mountbatten family crest had to be altered, but the new reproductions were ready before we left for India. Not only was the stationery stamped with the new crest, it was also engraved on our crockery and hardware, ashtrays included.

Only forty-eight hours before we were due to depart Lord Louis almost changed his mind. The R.A.F. told him that his favourite York MW102, the aircraft he had travelled the world in, would not be available for him. Lord Louis told the Group Captain who relayed the message, 'If you can't supply the plane then I won't be going out to India. One of the conditions I made was that I should go out there in the York.'

Without further ado the York was made immediately available. It was as well it was. We had sixty-six pieces of luggage to pack aboard!

Lord Louis trusted that plane like he trusted his most faithful

Labrador. It was a converted Lancaster bomber. Its fuselage had been furnished to form two sitting rooms, with a table and chairs that were screwed down to the floor in one section, and pull-down beds that also served as settees in the other. There was a specially equipped galley for cooking. Extra fuel tanks had been put in for the long journey.

Not once had the plane been involved in any kind of accident, although I do remember one anxious moment when we were flying out of Lisbon in a storm. Even Lord Louis, who had the ability to keep cool in any situation, could not help showing a moment's consternation. From the tail end came a sudden explosion and one of the crew staggered into the main body of the fuselage, covered in what we first thought was blood. In fact it was tomato ketchup – a bottle had exploded all over him as he prepared a meal in the galley!

Lord Louis was pretty cagey about going to India. His feelings were that the Indians wouldn't take kindly to his presence and he saw little hope of reconciling the opposing Hindus, Muslims and Sikhs. Only the previous year there had been the most terrible bloodshed when 6,000 people were slaughtered in the Calcutta riots. Lord Louis had indicated to the King that his chances of bringing a peaceful settlement to India were remote and it would be bad for His Majesty to have a member of his family fail.

The King replied, 'But think how good it will be for the monarchy if you succeed.'

It was a fine, spring-like day when we left Northolt, but Lord Louis still held misgivings. As we climbed aboard the plane he told his aide-de-camp, Lieutenant-Commander Peter Howes, 'I don't want to go. They don't want me out there. We'll probably come home with bullets in our backs.'

I don't think Lord Louis, even with his great foresight, ever envisaged that the time would come when his name was as legendary in India as it was in Burma. The Indian people loved him; they learned that he was a man of immense wisdom, as Gandhi, Nehru and many other leaders came to acknowledge.

Lord Louis' 'swearing-in' as Viceroy was an occasion marked with almost as much pomp and pageantry as a coronation. To all intents and purposes it was a coronation, for Lord Louis was to occupy a throne from which he would govern all India. The gold and crimson throne was mounted on a plinth in the marble palace of Durbar Hall in New Delhi. It was a monument of great architectural beauty.

I dressed Lord Louis for the ceremony in a private chamber of the hall and this is how an observer described the scene:

In one of the private chambers of the great house, a man contemplated the white full-dress admiral's uniform his employer would wear to take possession of Viceroy's House's majestic precincts. No flaring turban graced his head. Charles Smith was not a product of the Punjab or Rajasthan, but of a country village in the south of England.

With a meticulous regard for detail acquired over a quarter of a century of service in Mountbatten's employ, Smith slipped the cornflower-blue silk sash of the world's most exclusive company, the Order of the Garter, through the right epaulette and stretched it taut across the uniform's breast. Then he looped the gold aiguillettes which marked the uniform's owner as a personal A.D.C. to King George VI through the right epaulette.

Finally, Smith took his employer's medal bar and the four major stars he would wear this morning from their velvet boxes. With respect and care he gave a last polish to their gleaming gold and silver enamel forms: the Order of the Garter, the Order of the Star of India, the Order of the Indian Empire, the Grand Cross of the Victorian Order.

Those rows of ribbons and crosses marking the milestones of Louis Mountbatten's career were, in their special fashion, the milestones along the course of Charles Smith's life as well. Since he had joined Mountbatten's service as third footman at the age of eighteen, Smith had walked in another man's shadow. In the great country houses of England, in the naval stations of the Empire, in the capitals of Europe, his employer's joys had been his, his triumphs, his victories, his sorrows, his griefs. During the war, he had joined the service and eventually followed Mountbatten to South-East Asia. There, from a spectator's seat in the City Hall of Singapore, Charles Smith had watched with tears of pride filling his eyes as Mountbatten, in another uniform he'd prepared, had effaced the worst humiliation Britain had ever endured by taking the surrender of almost three-quarters of a million Japanese soldiers, sailors and airmen.

Smith stepped back to contemplate his work. No one in the world was more demanding when it came to dressing a uniform than Mountbatten, and this was not a morning to make a mistake. Smith unbuttoned the jacket and sash, and gingerly lifted it from the dress dummy on which it rested. He eased it over his own shoulders and turned to a mirror for a final check. There, for a brief and poignant moment before that mirror, he was out of the shadows. For just a second, Charles Smith, too, could dream he was Viceroy of India.

Those words, taken from *Freedom at Midnight* by Larry Collins and Dominique Lapierre, bring back many memories for me and I congratulate the writer: I did put myself in Lord Louis' place that day, as I am sure any valet would have done. In any event, it was a proud moment for me. Lord Louis, as he took the throne, with Lady Louis by his side, looked resplendent. They both did.

In the early weeks of Lord Louis' rule there was a curfew in the capital because of the conflicts of the religious sects. Lord Louis invited all the leaders to Government House in turn so that he could try and resolve the problems before Independence was declared.

It meant, eventually, partition and the declaration of the state of Pakistan, which had not been His Lordship's original intention. But in the passing of time he realized that this was an inevitable step.

One morning Gandhi, the man Winston Churchill had called 'a half-naked fakir', came to the house, recognizable only because of the loin cloth that he wore. He stayed on for afternoon tea, which was arranged on the lawn with scones and sandwiches served by our Indian houseboys – my staff having enlarged considerably at Government House! The Indian leader did not touch either the cakes or sandwiches, but chose to eat a bowl of goat's curd which he had brought with him. He even persuaded Lord Louis to sample a mouthful! His Lordship bravely swallowed it, but gracefully declined the offer of more.

Once back in his room he said, 'I can think of a lot of things I would rather do before eating goat's curd again!'

But of Gandhi there was nothing but homage. Said Lord Louis, 'He is one of the most remarkable men I have met in my life, Charles. There is not another man to compare with him in the world. No man has such faith.'

Gandhi visited Government House on two further occasions, but Pandit Nehru was a more frequent visitor and so too was another of the politicians, Sardar Patel. Their conferences would be conducted in Lord Louis' office, the picture rails of which were hung with his wartime regimental plaques, which were later copied and hung at Broadlands.

It was Mr Nehru who had recommended Lord Louis for the post of Viceroy.

His Lordship was soon to make his mark, and so was Lady Louis who set out like a missionary to explore the backward areas where poverty and sickness were prevalent and to give her help. Socially, there were also many important engagements she had to conduct as Vicereine at Government House – state banquets, garden parties and conferences.

Lady Louis normally relied on fashions from London and Paris, but when her wardrobe ran low in Delhi she asked me to find something new for her to wear. I took one of the cars out into Delhi and went in search of a dress shop for her. I was fortunate enough to find one that was run by two Europeans, and having taken along one of Lady Louis' dresses as a sample for style and measurement, they were able to find at least a dozen garments that were possibly suitable for her. I drove them back to the house and one of the owners came with me to arrange a special fitting for Lady Louis. Her Ladyship congratulated me, 'Charles, you're a marvel. Where did you find them?'

My room on the compound was at least ten minutes' walk from where Lord and Lady Louis were situated and to cut my journey I managed to acquire an old motorbike which I only managed to ride for four days before I was banned from using it! Lord Louis' household controller, one of the military staff, reprimanded me.

Princess Elizabeth and
Philip in Romsey

The 1953 Coronation.
Pamela is on the left, Lord
Lady Brabourne on the

Lee Lodge, Broadlands, where Violet and I lived before we moved to the stable yard cottage nearer the main house when I became butler in 1954

The lounge of our stable yard cottage

'Get rid of that infernal machine right away!' he told me. 'It makes too much din.'

Off-duty hours were spent at the swimming pool which was set on the edge of a plantation. It was a sanctuary for the most exquisite birds – parrots, parakeets and other exotic, colourful species. I would study them for hours.

Up country we would often come across territories completely overrun by monkeys. These areas were not safe to cross alone on foot without carrying a large stick of some kind. On one occasion Lady Louis took the children there for a picnic, but the monkeys moved in and poached all our food, chattering with triumph as they departed!

The Indian Government asked Lord Louis to stay on as Governor-General after Independence was declared a year ahead of schedule. His Lordship accepted and he held the office for ten months, a period during which both he and his wife were to see much sadness before peace finally settled over this huge continent.

Fresh riots broke out in the remote territories and Lady Louis volunteered to work with the homeless and the refugees, visiting camps and organizing vaccinations and proper sanitation.

Then came a very bitter blow that could well have erupted into civil war. A Hindu fanatic assassinated Gandhi in the grounds of Birla House in Delhi.

Lord Mountbatten recalled that dreadful, black day in India's history when he later said (in *the Life and Times of Lord Mountbatten* by John Terraine):

To say I was appalled conveys nothing – I was absolutely numbed and petrified. I went round at once to Birla House. There was a large crowd round the house already, and inside it most of the members of the Government – everyone in tears.

Gandhi looked very peaceful in death, but I dreaded what his death might bring.

As I went into the house where his body was lying, someone in the crowd shouted out:

'It was a Muslim who did it!'

I turned immediately and said:

'You fool, don't you know it was a Hindu?'

Of course, I didn't know – no one knew at that stage; but I did know this: if it was a Muslim, we were lost. There would be civil war without fail. Thank God it wasn't! It turned out to be a Hindu extremist.

What terrified me most now was the thought that these people might strike again – at Nehru, or Sardar Patel. There had been a growing coolness between these two great men. I took this opportunity, then and there, in front of Gandhi's body, of bringing them together again, as I knew he would have wished. They embraced each other in tears. I felt this act was a symbol of Gandhi's power, even after death. You still feel it strongly in India today.

Such was the wisdom of my master, Lord Louis. No wonder he and Lady Louis were loved and honoured by the Indian people throughout their lives.

8

A Royal Marriage

knew them as children, I played and conspired with them in their
ames. Now I was to organize the one adventure that I hadn't
nticipated, and I'm sure they hadn't either – their honeymoon.

I don't think it ever occurred to me that Princess Elizabeth and
rince Philip would one day fall in love and marry. It was a fairytale
omance and one that I'm certain the benevolent Uncle Dickie
ncouraged. I was elated for them when the official announcement of
1eir engagement was made. I felt a rush of pride that I had figured,
`fractionally in their Royal lives.

But now I was to play a much more important part and one that
ad to be undertaken in great secrecy. For Prince Philip and Princess
lizabeth were to spend the first part of their honeymoon at Broad-
1nds, as Lord and Lady Louis had done on their marriage.

Every day leading up to the Westminster Abbey wedding on 20
Iovember, 1947 the world's press speculated on the bridal couple's
oneymoon destination. They never guessed that the couple would
3ttle for the autumnal English countryside of Broadlands!

Lord and Lady Louis, who flew home from India specially for the
vedding, placed me in charge of the honeymoon arrangements at the
ouse, along with the butler Frank Randall, and I had been sent
ome ahead of them in order to start the preparations.

It was a day that London, and the nation, was never to forget. And neither was I. It was the most glittering event of the forties, with the monarchies of Europe and other more distant sovereigns, together with a multitude of princes and princesses, grand dukes and duchesses, heads of state and peers of the realm all filling the pews of Westminster Abbey.

When, finally, the fanfares had died away and the great wedding ceremony was over, I left Lord and Lady Louis at Buckingham Palace. They were returning immediately to India, leaving me to hasten on my special mission to Broadlands to await the arrival of the honeymoon couple.

Like any woman who might have found herself in that position Lady Louis was anxious to ensure that everything at the house was spick and span.

'Now, Charles,' she said, 'you will take good care of them, won't you?'

I assured Her Ladyship that their every need would be taken care of and I added, 'Nothing will be any different, Your Ladyship, from the way it always is.'

Lady Louis frowned – but then caught my meaning.

'I'm sorry, Charles,' she said, 'I didn't mean to question what you were doing. You're absolutely right – nothing should be different. Their Royal Highnesses would not want that. If the house is run as it always is, then I'm sure there will be nothing to worry about.'

I had already instructed the staff, and Frank Randall the butler agreed with me, that we were all to go about our normal duties as though a honeymoon was spent at Broadlands every day.

'If we attempt to do something out of the ordinary, or make a special fuss, their Royal Highnesses will detect it and they might feel uncomfortable about it,' I lectured, calling together all our maids and servants in the stewards' room.

My experience in service had led me to the conclusion that special attempts to please or to arrange something differently invariably had a nasty habit of going wrong. Untried, special dishes might be prepared that perhaps took too long to cook, keeping guests on edge and hungry. Similarly with wines. It was never wise to experiment on guests. Nor was it sensible to change staff routines or procedures at the last minute.

Having said all of that, however, it was difficult not to feel the air of expectancy that existed among us at Broadlands that special day. I think we were much more nervous than the honeymooners themselves when they arrived early in the evening in a black Rolls-Royce bearing the Royal standard and accompanied by two detectives, their personal maid and valet in a second car.

Princess Elizabeth looked very relaxed in a tweed costume, and Prince Philip, now wearing a grey suit, gave me the impression that he was relieved that at last they had been able to escape from the pomp and ceremony.

'Good evening, Charles,' said Princess Elizabeth, shaking my hand as I bowed to the couple in the entrance hall.

Prince Philip grinned, recognizing his former darts partner in the Kensington Palace pantry, and said, 'How good to see you, Charles. Are you still going for the bull's eye?'

My heart warmed to see the Royal couple and I felt a great honour in being given the opportunity to look after them on their honeymoon.

They were to occupy the Portico Room, a room of regal furnishings, classic oil paintings and a magnificent canopied four-poster bed. The windows looked out on to the most breathtaking views over the Test River valley, across broad meadows to sweeping wooded hills beyond.

We all realized how essential it was for us to respect their total privacy and the staff were asked to make their presence known only when the service bell rang.

Detective Inspector Perkins, who was in charge of security, had made arrangements with the local police so that proper precautions were taken at all the lodge gates leading into the estate. He predicted that it would be only a matter of hours before the press discovered the location of the bridal couple. But nothing came to disturb the Royal couple. They took long walks, hand in hand, over the estate, or went riding on a pair of Lord Louis' ponies. They shared His Lordship's passion for horses and spent many hours in and around the stables.

They went to bed before midnight and rose quite early. They breakfasted lightly on grapefruit and boiled eggs, but their appetites were keener at lunchtime after trekking over the estate. Our 'menu' allowed the Royal couple a wide choice of dishes, from fresh salmon, trout and plaice if their tastes were inclined towards fish, to roasts of venison, beef, lamb or veal. And, of course, there was pheasant and other game. Champagne cocktails were served with caviare and a selection of canapés.

The Prince and Princess would take their meals in the main dining room, which we made cosier for them be erecting a small, circular table in front of the log fire, and arranging settees and softer furnishings to give a 'closed-in' effect. Dinner by candlelight also helped to create a more romantic and intimate atmosphere.

Fresh flowers were cut daily to decorate the table, and the bone crockery, silver cutlery and crystal glass were the finest from our pantry. Everything was delicately arranged, without the slightest fuss. We were anxious to ensure that the Royal couple's honeymoon was as quiet, private and simple as they obviously wanted it to be.

The memories must have been very precious for them, because in the years to come they always regarded Broadlands with such immense affection and they used it as a retreat from the pressures and protocol thrust upon them by the State.

I sent a letter to Lord and Lady Louis in Delhi assuring them that everything had worked out perfectly in relation to the honeymoon arrangements and I received a note of congratulation.

After the Royal departure things became very quiet at Broadlands and I was asked to 'stand-in', with Violet accompanying me as parlour maid, in service to Lady Louis' cousin, Lady Brecknock, whose home was at Liphook. We spent four very happy months there and Her Ladyship treated us with great kindness and consideration.

Towards the end of June 1948 it was time to return to Broadlands, to prepare for Lord and Lady Louis' homecoming. Their mission was complete.

I travelled to Northolt to greet them as they disembarked from the ever-reliable York. They were in good health, but I must confess my own well-being shook a little when I saw the mountains of luggage that was being stacked on the tarmac from the plane's hold. There must have been at least a dozen more pieces than when they set out.

When I came to unpack all the cases at Broadlands, a task that took me several days, I was left in no doubt of the high regard in which the Indian people must have held Lord and Lady Louis. The cases brimmed with treasures and souvenirs, many of which had been given to Lord and Lady Louis to mark the celebration of their Silver Wedding anniversary which they had spent in Delhi. One of the gifts I recall unwrapping was a silver replica of an Indian palace, the interior decorated with an illuminated miniature wedding day picture of Lord and Lady Louis.

Even on the day of their departure Pandit Nehru had apparently presented them with a silver salver on behalf of the Cabinet and Governors of all the Provinces of India.

But gifts weren't the only prizes that Lord and Lady Louis brought home with them. Along too came Abdul and Wally Beg, two Indian houseboys, who had served the Mountbattens all through their stay in Delhi.

'They have heard so much about Broadlands that I thought they would like to see it,' explained Lord Louis. 'Besides, Charles, you will find they will be of great help to you.'

Indeed they were; they took a lot of work off my shoulders in the year that they stayed with us, particularly when several of the Indian leaders visited England and stayed with us at Broadlands.

Pandit Nehru was one, and his photograph appeared so frequently in the press that his black mandarin-style jacket inspired a new fashion!

Mr Nehru was a yoga fanatic and even when he was at Broadlands he didn't forsake his regular morning exercises. Before having breakfast he would meditate standing on his head. When I first found him in that position, wearing only a white singlet and trunks, I almost dropped my tray in astonishment. It was no hardship to him. He could conduct a perfectly relaxed conversation in this position.

'Please put the tray down on the table,' said Mr Nehru. Detecting I was flustered, he added, 'You should try it, Charles. It is very good for you.'

I said, 'Yes, Sir, I imagine so, but I don't think I have the ability to stand on my head.'

'Nonsense,' said Mr Nehru, bouncing back onto his feet like a rubber jack-in-the-box. 'Everyone can do it.'

He demonstrated it once more, folding his arms and poising his feet perfectly above his head. Then he laughed and broke his posture to take time to peruse the tray I had prepared for him with tea, grapefruit and cereal.

His Lordship bumped into me one morning when I was on my way to Mr Nehru's bedroom at the same hour and he followed me through.

When we got to the doorway I knocked, and Mr Nehru said, 'Please come in.'

His Lordship looked over my shoulder and gasped, for the Indian leader was again standing on his head.

'Does he do this every morning, Charles?' boomed His Lordship so that Mr Nehru would hear.

'Oh yes, m'Lord,' I said.

'Funny fellow,' said Lord Louis, 'that explains why he sees the world upside down!'

Mr Nehru's confidante, Mr Krishna Menon, was another welcome figure at Broadlands. Dining with Her Ladyship one evening, our guest asked for some tea. When Lady Louis poured it, she complained, 'Charles, I'm afraid this tea is a bit weak.'

Examining Mr Menon's cup, I realized that it was only hot water. I had forgotten to put any tea leaves into the pot!

'If you are running short, we have plenty in India I can get for you!' laughed Mr Menon.

He even managed to smile when he left some important papers at the house, which meant returning to Broadlands all the way from London the same night. When I saw him sprawled out snoozing in the ante-room at 7.00 a.m. having seen his departure six hours before, I was astounded. I disturbed Lord Louis.

'I think, m'Lord, I have just seen a ghost. The ghost of Mr Menon. He is asleep in an armchair downstairs,' I said.

His Lordship got out of bed in one stride.

'You must be mistaken, Charles. I saw him off myself,' he said, putting on his dressing gown.

His Lordship went to investigate, but quickly returned.

'No, Charles, it isn't a ghost. It's Mr Menon all right – he's forgotten some papers.'

The nightwatchman had let Mr Menon back into the house and when I served him a pot of tea to refresh him, I said, 'This time, Sir, I did remember the tea.'

He placed his hand on my arm and said, 'Think no more about it, Charles. I'm not infallible either, otherwise I would not have had to come all the way back here!'

9

Domestic Duties

There was a daily set drill for all of us on the domestic staff at Broadlands. A personal maid would take care of Lady Louis' needs and her wardrobe, while I would be entirely responsible for Lord Louis' sector.

Lord and Lady Louis shared communicating rooms, one furnished with a double bed and the other with a single bed. Each had their own bathroom.

Her Ladyship's bedroom and adjoining sitting room were both predominantly white, with chintz curtains hung in one room and cream-coloured drapings in the other. Antiques and figurines adorned the recesses and a collection of Salvador Dali's sketches, which Her Ladyship greatly valued, were hung on the walls. Dali had also painted an unusual portrait of Lady Louis, with snakes ringing her hair like a turban.

His Lordship's suite was a total contrast. It was splashed with a very warm and pleasing coral. Curtains, quilts and chair coverings were all the same colour. Replacement sets were ordered so that Lord Louis could take them anywhere in the world he came to make his home. So not only would I find myself packing his personal belongings, but curtains, bed covers and runners too! They had even gone to India with him, His Lordship coming to explain: 'They give me the atmosphere of home, Charles. A feeling of Broadlands . . .'

When Lady Louis was away on her own travels, His Lordship did not alter his rigid daily procedure. He would start his day at 7.50 a.m. precisely, affording himself, as he would say, a fifty-minute lie-in from the 7.00 a.m. rise he made whenever he was on active Naval duty.

Every morning I would rouse him by drawing the curtains and switching on a transistor radio he kept by his bedside. Lord Louis liked to listen to the 8.00 a.m. world news on B.B.C., and then he would study the morning newspapers – in those days he took *The Times*, the *Daily Express* and the *Daily Mirror* (he loved the cartoon strips!), before turning to his morning's mail.

By one glance at a letter he could predict its contents and he would open only those communications he wanted to read. The rest of the letters were left for his secretary to deal with.

If, in this routine, we ran a minute late, I would invariably get the blame.

'Oh, Charles, damn and blast it,' he would mumble, 'that means to say I am going to be a minute late all day.'

He would slip on a dressing gown over his plain-coloured pyjamas and then contemplate breakfast. His appetite was usually good at that time of the day. Sometimes he would have eggs and bacon, other mornings he would prefer boiled eggs, but he liked fish too, especially kippers and fish cakes.

Our Austrian-born chef, Joe Brinz, had a marvellous recipe for fish cakes and Lord Louis adored them. I had to get instructions on how to make them, so that when we were abroad I could cook them for his breakfast.

His Lordship, a pillar of physical fitness, never had a weight problem. His energies burned away all the calories. But there were certain foods he was most finicky about, and top of that list was the common tomato.

Lord Louis nursed a strong loathing of tomatoes. He didn't like their taste, and nor, for that matter, did he like their colour or their shape! The mere sight of them would vex him.

He pulled me up once for serving ham sandwiches to a party of guests and decorating the salver with lettuce leaves and sliced tomatoes!

Sliding over to my side, he whispered, 'Charles, what on earth are those damn tomatoes doing there?'

I said, 'M'Lord, I'm sorry. I know you don't like tomatoes yourself, but some of our guests probably do. Shall I continue to serve them?'

'Yes, Charles, I suppose so . . . but really, how can they eat such wretched things?'

Her Ladyship would prepare a weekly menu – a job that passed to me in her absence – and the card would be taken down to the kitchen to Joe Brinz so that he could order the necessary supplies.

Joe, who had been trained in the traditional French schools of high cuisine, could make a banquet out of bangers and mash! He knew all Lord Louis' likes and dislikes, but he would frequently garnish a variety of main dishes with mushrooms. His Lordship preferred the mushrooms to be served separately and he would tut, 'I'd rather have them laid out on a slice of toasted bread.'

Caviare was Lord Louis' real passion. Many Royals knew his weakness and would send him the odd tin. Supplies would also come from Fortnum and Mason's. Sometimes, if he only had a small jar and there wasn't sufficient for his guests, he would have a quiet, pre-dinner snack in his bedroom.

Equally, he loved grouse and pheasant, but once broke a tooth on a pheasant leg sandwich because the maid had left it unboned!

He enjoyed all sorts of nuts, too, and I would often find myself in the grounds in the autumn searching for walnuts and cob-nuts as they dropped fresh from the trees.

'You had better get them in, Charles, before the squirrels snaffle the lot,' His Lordship would remind me.

Lord Louis was proud of the produce that Broadlands itself provided. Butter, milk, eggs, fruit, and vegetables all came from the home farm on the estate with its own dairy herd.

For his Lordship's personal needs I would be entrusted with a monthly £50 'float'. I would buy his hairbrushes, combs, lotions and after-shave, and if I overspent I would be reimbursed.

When I drew money for him I would put it into his bedroom drawer rather than his wallet, which would annoy His Lordship.

'For God's sake, Charles, why can't you put the notes straight into my wallet? That's where I need them!' he would say.

My answer was simple. 'A man's wallet is his most personal possession. Even a valet hasn't got the right to touch it.'

'Nonsense!' retorted Lord Louis. 'If I trust you with my life, I trust you with my wallet.'

Loose change in his pockets irritated him, especially odd coppers and sixpences which he would pull out when having to give a tip to someone. I would replace the lower denominations with florins and half-crowns.

His Lordship was thrifty, especially in relation to his personal needs. He always kept an eye on his clothing bills!

He didn't smoke and he would give me his 200 duty-free cigarette allowance when we passed through Customs together. Occasionally he smoked cigars, but these were passing phases and he was never tempted to make it a habit.

His Lordship wasn't a drinker either. When he went out to banquets he might sip a glass of champagne or sherry, but his knowledge of wines was lacking because, as he said, he had no interest in them. Indeed, he would prefer a special lemonade that I concocted for him. I made it with fresh lemons, citric acid, tartaric acid and Epsom salts which I would mix into boiling water and leave to cool for twenty-four hours. I would then bottle it, and if Lord Louis was going out to dinner, I would send one to the hosts, so that His Lordship would not have to drink table wine.

Guests at Broadlands could, of course, always have any wine or champagne of their choice. Our cellars were very well stocked, but many visitors finished up drinking His Lordship's lemonade in preference!

I think there was only one alcoholic drink that Lord Louis enjoyed and that he regarded as something of a treat. It was orange brandy flip, which I would make with Martell brandy, Seville oranges, lemon, cream, raw eggs, and loaf sugar. Sometimes His Lordship would have a glass to line his stomach at mid-morning, and he would enjoy another one after dinner.

Naval men have a reputation for drinking, but I don't think Lord Louis would have become an Admiral if that had been a necessary qualification. The Navy might have felt he was really letting the side down had they known that he never touched rum and that his favourite drink was no stronger than a chocolate milk shake that he would have every day instead of afternoon tea!

Dinner parties at Broadlands were always special affairs and I would deploy the pantry staff to clean the silver and wipe over the Royal Doulton china. If thirteen guests were expected the dining room table would be split at the tail end and three guests would find themselves divided from the rest of the table by a six-inch gap.

Lady Louis said, 'We're not superstitious at all, Charles, but some of our guests might be!'

Great trouble would be taken to get to know if any of our special guests had any particular fads. We had a 'grapevine' running between the British Royal palaces, and the houses of Sweden, Spain, Holland, and Greece, to establish tastes in cuisine and wines. Prior to any Royal visit I would call a member of the opposing staff and get a 'briefing'.

It was this 'tic tac' service that led to Lord Louis discovering that my home-brewed lemonade was served to him wherever he went.

'Good gracious,' he said at St James's Palace one night when sipping his drink, 'this tastes exactly like the lemonade my valet makes.'

'Yes, Sir,' said the Palace footman, 'it's the same make!'

Special culinary dishes for vegetarians provided little problem for Joe Brinz, who was also a master at making Indian curries and could equally conjure superb Greek food whenever King Paul of Greece stayed with us.

Even the monarchs had their little eccentricities. King Alfonso of Spain would always like a rare steak for breakfast, while the King of Sweden loved brandy pancakes which he would insist on cooking himself!

Other important guests also had their funny ways. Novelist Barbara Cartland, irrespective of the nourishment of the cuisine provided, would distribute jars of vitamin and rejuvenating pills to Lord Louis, the family, the staff, and the dogs!

'Take these,' she would say, 'they will give you a new lease of life!'

Most guests would offer us tips at the end of their stay; it was

CHIEF OF THE DEFENCE STAFF

MINISTRY OF DEFENCE

STOREY'S GATE, LONDON S.W.1

TELEPHONE WHITEHALL 7000

31st October 1962

Dear Charles,

The King of Norway has written
to say how much he enjoyed his stay
at Broadlands and how much he
appreciated the way he was looked
after in the house.

As I had to leave in a hurry and
he meant to give me the money for the
tips he has now sent me £7, which is
for yourself, Mrs. Smith, Mrs. Yeates,
and perhaps Mrs. Jones. I will leave
it to you to divide up as you think
best.

Yours sincerely

Mountbatten of Burma

3rd July 1961.

Dear Charles,

If the routine this weekend is
more normal than last weekend I shall
be staying at Britwell Salome with
Lady Pamela, from Friday night, and
Sergeant Wright will drive from Oxford
(where he will have been driving me on
official business) direct to Broadlands
for the weekend, and to pick up the
farm produce and flowers first thing
Monday morning.

He has to be at Britwell at about
0900 and will have to leave therefore
at about 0730,

Please make sure that he takes with
him the little gold powder box, which I
am going to give to Madame Letellier,
which I asked to be finished not later
than 8th July.

He may also have to take a Chestnut
tree for planting at Paimpol, but this
depends on the arrangements which Commander
Kennon makes with Commander Webb.

yours sincerely

Mountbatten of Burma

ables at Broadlands

g the finishing touches to Lord Louis' uniform

February 1960. Lady Pamela's wedding to David Hicks. Back row, left to right: Lady Brabourne (second from left), Lord Louis, Mrs Hicks, Prince Philip, Lady Louis, Lord Brabourne, who was best man. Middle row: The Duchess of Gloucester, Princess Margaret, H.M. Queen Elizabeth the Queen Mother, the bridegroom and bride, Queen Louise of Sweden, the Duchess of Kent, Princess Alexandra of Kent. Front row: Amanda Knatchbull; bridesmaids; Victoria usually a matter of £2 or £3, and Lord and Lady Louis didn't object to any of the staff accepting these nominal rewards.

The King of Norway once forgot to leave anything at all and was so conscious-stricken that he sent £7 to Lord Louis, who asked me to distribute the money amongst the staff.

An Arab sheikh who only stayed for two days tipped me £100 in £10 notes and I thought I should tell His Lordship about it.

'Put it in your pocket and keep your big trap shut, Charles!' advised His Lordship.

Most of the distinguished figures who came to Broadlands were invited to plant saplings in the grounds: copper beech trees, mulberries, oaks, and other varieties. It became something of a ritual and I think that every member of the British Royal family, as well as the Royal houses of Sweden and Spain, put down roots at Broadlands! So, too, did the Duke and Duchess of Windsor, the King of Thailand and Charlie Chaplin.

I filmed most of these ceremonies on an 8 m.m. cine camera in order to keep a permanent record for posterity, and His Lordship compiled a location chart for each tree planted on the estate, showing who had taken part in the proceedings.

Lord and Lady Louis were always the most genial of hosts, setting out to please their guests in every aspect. They would derive enormous pleasure from it all, especially when their guests made full use of all the facilities that Broadlands offered.

Those guests who didn't go shooting or riding would find relaxation fishing on the Test; the river was regarded as one of the best in the country for salmon and trout. Lord Louis occasionally went fishing himself, and he would take along his fishkeeper Bernard Aldrich to keep an eye on the float! We would normally go down to a distant reach of the river in my three-wheeler Messerschmitt car, Lord Louis clutching the fishing rods, which poked through the open window.

My three-wheeler held a certain fascination for Lady Louis. Its perspex roof was rather like an aeroplane cockpit. Her Ladyship once had to attend an important charity gala and hitched a lift there in my Messerschmitt in preference to the Rolls. When Her Ladyship stepped out of the little bubble car, dodging between an august line of Rolls-Royces, Daimlers, Bentleys and Mercedes, there were gasps of surprise. No one expected the guest of honour to arrive in such a modest vehicle, but then Lady Louis didn't stand on ceremony. And neither, for that matter, did Lord Louis.

They were alike in so many ways. They were both individualistic, they were both crusaders. They sacrificed much for their beliefs and their objectives, but they safeguarded the one thing that was vital to them: their marriage and family.

I was convinced that their unity gave them the strength for their public lives. They influenced and inspired each other. They were happily married in the true sense of the word. Time was their greatest enemy, because the demands that were made on them allowed scarce hours that they could spend together.

Occasionally they had their tiffs, usually when the time factor intervened on their plans. A last-minute appointment would arise to sabotage their domestic arrangements, as on the night Lord Louis was called to the Admiralty when Her Ladyship had organized a West End theatre party.

'There he goes, Charles. There's no point in trying to stop him,' said Lady Louis forlornly, left to explain to her guests the reason for His Lordship's absence.

Sometimes they would take different points of view on world situations, but they always respected one another's opinions. They wasted no time in debating trivial matters. When disagreements did occur between them, they were quickly remedied and there was no antagonism harboured by either side. Lord Louis was not vindictive or malicious; and neither was Lady Louis. Whenever something was wrong, they would clear the air rather than let their feelings fester.

The success of marriage depends very largely on matched upbringing. Of that I am convinced. People should never marry out of their station, otherwise discontent will soon emerge. Lord and Lady Louis were perfectly matched. They were both highly intelligent and Lord Louis' background blended with Lady Louis' environment and wealth.

So much today is written about Women's Lib, but Lady Louis has made mockery of their war cries by personal example. She travelled the world helping refugees and impoverished people while occupy-

ing the role of wife and mother with a depth of femininity and love
that encased her family and helped ensure its unity. Lord Louis
admired her independent free spirit and all her skills in being able to
lead and organize people, for these were qualities he recognized
within himself.

His love for her was abundantly evident. Not once did he ever
forget Her Ladyship's birthday, or their anniversary. Each anniversary gift was date-stamped so its actual commemoration would
always be known to them. His Lordship would personally supervise
the ordering of these presents; some were custom-made by crafts-
men, including an oval-shaped silver gilt clock on which the digits
of their names 'Dickie Edwina' replaced the twelve numerals on its
face.

Lord Louis liked Roman numerals and these were embossed on
many of the other anniversary presents, as well as forming the chain of a
beautiful gold necklace he had commissioned for his wife in Paris.

Lady Louis' thoughts were similarly sentimental and she would
relish spoiling His Lordship with unexpected presents: perhaps a
book, or a classical record, or a pair of new cuff links. Nor did she
forget the important occasions. She had a diamond and sapphire
replica made of His Lordship's Garter Star, an idea she originally
pursued when His Lordship was created a Grand Commander of the
Victorian Order.

They were both very generously disposed towards the staff, and so
too were their daughters.

Lord Louis would always return from trips on which I did not
accompany him with a personal gift for me. Sometimes it would be
a lighter, or an ashtray, or perhaps a piece of porcelain which he
knew I collected. He also presented me with three signed, framed
portraits of himself taken at State ceremonies when I had been
responsible for his robing. Kindliness flowed through his veins like
a river. And he always took a personal interest in the welfare of all
his staff, and their families. He sent me a very kind note when my
mother died.

Seeking a favour from Lord Louis was a matter of knowing when
he was in a good mood, and I could always discern when he was
pleased with life because he had a habit of clenching his hands. And I

BROADLANDS.
ROMSEY.
HAMPSHIRE.

15ᵗʰ Feb 1968

My dear Charles,

I am so sorry to hear
of your mother's death and send
you my sincere condolences.

I know how I felt when I
lost my mother and you have all
my sympathy

Yours sincerely

Mountbatten of Burma

would say to myself, 'If you've got something on your mind to ask him, now is the time to nobble him!'

When provoked His Lordship had a fierce bark and there were times when he could be obstreperous, but there was no lasting vindictiveness.

Through all the years I was to spend with him he never sacked one employee, and there must have been more than 120 between the various houses, Broadlands estate and the farmlands. When someone let him down or did not perform their duties satisfactorily, he would be disappointed, but he would always give that person a second chance. For example, on H.M.S. *Kelly* during the war a man deserted his post and Lord Louis chose to caution the man instead of punishing him; the penalty he could have rightfully imposed was death.

While holding such authority His Lordship did not inflict his own views on other people. Socially, he always encouraged free discussion and that augured well for me!

We had another of our 'barneys' when I bought my first car. It was second-hand and I decided to buy it on hire purchase. When Lord Louis found out what I had done he was furious.

'You're a bloody fool, Charles, don't you realize you will be paying double the price for it in the end with all the interest that is put on? Go and cancel the agreement right away and get a cheque from my secretary's office. You can pay me back as and when you can afford it, and I won't charge you any interest at all.'

I was very grateful to His Lordship and when I came to change the car a couple of years later he offered a further loan to cover the balance of the exchange.

I remember I still owed Lord Louis £180 when I went into hospital for an operation on a nagging duodenal ulcer, and as a precautionary measure I had Lord Louis made a beneficiary to one of my life insurance policies.

'Good heavens, Charles! What on earth did you do that for?' he exclaimed, shaking his head in bewilderment.

'M'Lord, at the end of the road I don't want to leave any debts behind,' I explained.

'That's very commendable, Charles,' said Lord Louis, beginning to smile, 'but I don't think I would have pressed the claim!'

2. WILTON CRESCENT.

LONDON. S. W. 1.

8th February, 1951.

Dear Charles,

      This is just a line to say that
I am so delighted to hear that your
operation has been a complete success. It
must naturally have left you very weak as
it was a very serious operation; but
apparently also a very necessary one.

      The main thing now is to get rest
and quiet and get strong again. As Her·
Ladyship is unlikely to be back before the
end of March, you have nothing to worry
about and can take it as easy as you like
for as long as you like. All I want is
that you should get well again.

      If you require anything in the way
of fruit from the garden, or milk or eggs
from the farm, ask your wife to let Commander
North know that I authorise any reasonable
supplies for you.

      I thought it would amuse you to know
that I bought two dozen vests or singlets

from the Admiralty supplies which are
available to Officers and Men on repayment.
With purchase tax these 24 singlets cost me
£3.2.0d.

I personally cannot see any difference
between them and the vests which Hawes and
Curtis proposed to supply for £2.7.6d each!
I thought that would amuse you as it does show
what prices the London shops are now charging.

yours truly

Mountbatten of Burma

10

A Brandy for Sir Winston!

Lord and Lady Louis were on the verge of becoming grandparents and they were naturally very thrilled at the prospect. Their eldest daughter, Lady Patricia, now the wife of Lord Brabourne, was expecting her first child and as the time approached for its birth the family were on tenterhooks. More especially so when Lady Patricia's husband had to go to Scotland just when the baby was due.

Wearing a worried gaze, Lady Louis cast her eyes in my direction and suddenly exclaimed, 'Charles! You will be ideal for a crisis like this. We need someone who won't flap!'

Her Ladyship asked me if I would mind moving into Kensington Palace to keep an eye on Lady Patricia who was staying with Lord Louis' mother, the Dowager Marchioness of Milford Haven.

'Don't worry, Charles,' Lady Louis tried to reassure me, 'we will have a bell wired through to your room and once my daughter goes into labour she will ring it. All you have to do then is to get the car out and drive her as fast as you can to the hospital.'

While I didn't exactly resemble a midwife, Lady Patricia was visibly relieved to see me when I arrived at Kensington Palace with my overnight grip.

'Everything is all right at the moment, Charles,' she said, 'but these things can start at any minute and it's better to be ready than sorry. I shall feel a lot safer with you here. It is very kind of you to volunteer.'

I nodded a little nervously. It was certainly a new experience for me and I wondered how many other valets had been called on in this way.

'I do hope we will get good warning, Lady Patricia,' I said, 'because I don't think I would be a very good midwife.'

For two nights I didn't sleep. My eyes were firmly fixed on the bell by my bedside.

Each morning Lady Patricia would pat her tummy and say, 'I'm sorry, Charles. It looks like we've got to wait yet another day.'

To pass the time of day and as a necessary diversionary exercise, I would take Lady Patricia out in the car shopping. On other afternoons I would drive her and the Dowager out to Richmond Park and to Kew Gardens to give them an outing.

By the end of the week, my nights still sleepless, my nerves were shattered. In my mind I posed the most absurd questions. Supposing the car wouldn't start at the vital moment? What if I couldn't get a taxi? And then, who would deliver the child if I couldn't wake the Dowager?

Breaking out in a cold sweat, I phoned Violet, my wife, to ask her advice.

'Don't be silly, Charles. If there's an emergency I'm sure there are plenty of other people at Kensington Palace you can knock up to help,' she said.

All of this wasn't good for my blood pressure and I breathed with untold relief when Lord Brabourne, his business in Scotland concluded, returned home to resume command of things.

'Thank you, Charles, for standing in,' he said appreciatively. 'I'm only sorry we dragged you out on a false alarm.'

'Sir,' I gasped, swiftly taking my leave, 'I'm so glad it was!'

A few days later the couple's son Norton Knatchbull was born at the King Edward VII Hospital for Officers: a thriving, bouncing mite of 7 lbs and more, the future Lord Romsey and master of Broadlands.

We all breathed with relief that his birth went so well. For when she was five months' pregnant Lady Patricia might well have lost her baby. She was charged and butted by the infamous Billy the Goat on the farm at Broadlands, but fortunately she was tossed into a hayrick which softened her landing and no lasting harm was caused. Billy the Goat had a fearful temper and this unprovoked attack was regarded by His Lordship as the last straw! Lord Louis, always protective of his family, found Billy a new home in the safe custody of the zoo.

In time I was to watch the progress of Norton, and that, too, of His Royal Highness Prince Charles, who was born less than a year later; but in the coming years I was to find myself commuting between London and Malta carrying out Lord Louis' errands.

Lord Louis was back in the one uniform he loved more than any other, the Navy's. He was never happier than when he was at sea.

Before undertaking his Indian mission, he had extracted a promise from Mr Attlee that he would be allowed to return to the Navy when his term of office was over. Now that promise was fulfilled with his appointment as Rear-Admiral, commanding the 1st Cruiser Squadron in Malta.

A year later, in 1949, he was promoted to Vice-Admiral before ultimately taking over as Commander-in-Chief of the Mediterranean Fleet as well as the N.A.T.O. Allied Forces, whose headquarters were set up on the island.

This was all very well, as I grumbled to Lord Louis, but my whole life seemed to be spent on altering his uniforms and stitching on the flashings of his new ranks!

I was also the odd man out in the entire Mediterranean Fleet, leapfrogging in civilian clothes from one battleship or aircraft carrier to another on the non-stop trail of Lord Louis.

There might be a letter to deliver, or a message from Broadlands to pass on, as well as routine matters.

When Lady Louis joined His Lordship in Malta, and they took residence at Admiralty House in Valletta, my wife Violet came out as Her Ladyship's maid. She travelled by passenger ship with a prize cargo for Lord Louis – two of his polo ponies, which were being ferried out by the stable groom Mr Arthur Birch. Once more Lord

28th July, 1954.

My dear Charles,

Will you please send out 2 more
medium size bottles of my usual hair
lotion by ordinary parcel post as I am
running short.

You probably know that I have 3
very small pairs of "stumpy" folding
half spectacles in small blue cases.
Only two of them came back after I was
last at Broadlands and Spiteri thinks
I may have left the third pair at
Broadlands, perhaps in the pockets of
one of the pairs of trousers I wore
while I was there. Would you have a
search through all my trousers and all
my pockets generally to see if you can
find them and if so please send them back.

I hope all goes well with you.

Yours truly

Mountbatten of Burma

Louis was forming a polo team on the island. He also took up aqualung diving, which he thoroughly enjoyed.

Violet and I stayed in a small hotel practically next door to Admiralty House and when the Fleet sailed out for one of its exercises His Lordship loaned us the use of his Riley car so that we could go sightseeing. We even took it across to the neighbouring island of Gozo.

In April 1950 we had to go back to England for a two-year spell when His Lordship was appointed to the Admiralty in London as Fourth Sea Lord.

Sadly, that September his mother died. She was eighty-seven and she had lived a grand life but she had suffered in later years from acute arthritis. She also chain-smoked – I remember she used to order cigarette-holders 100 at a time! – which caused a dreadful cough, but in all of this she never complained. She was a very scholarly woman who was forever delving into books, and she was always forthcoming in passing on fresh knowledge to her family. She would also recount, with vivid description, her memories of her grandmother, the formidable Queen Victoria.

The Dowager was very annoyed, when guessing the end was near, that she didn't die at what she thought was the predetermined moment. Lord and Lady Louis, Princess Louise and Princess Alice and all other close members of the family went to pay their last respects. The Dowager said she let them down because she hung on to life a little longer and they all had to troup back a second time!

She would wake in the mornings and be astonished to find she was still alive.

'Am I still here? I'm not supposed to be,' she would protest.

When she finally departed, the family were heartbroken, the grandchildren especially.

In later years when a biographical book on his parents was published, Lord Louis sent me a copy and wrote inside, 'To Charles Smith, who knew my mother for 20 years and worked directly for her for four months.'

Only eighteen months after the Dowager's passing, King George VI died suddenly while Princess Elizabeth and Prince Philip were on holiday in Kenya. The Royal family, and nation, were stunned.

RICHARD HOUGH

Louis & Victoria

THE FIRST MOUNTBATTENS

To Charles Smith who knew my mother for 20 years and worked directly for her for 4 months

from

Mountbatten of Burma

A. F.

HUTCHINSON OF LONDON

When the period of mourning was over, Britain needed a tonic and the Coronation of Princess Elizabeth as Queen provided it. A festive air swept through cities, towns and villages in what was surely to be the spectacle of a lifetime. In London hundreds of thousands of people thronged the processional route and even the unkindly rain could not dampen the enthusiasm.

With a glut of monarchs, dukes, princes and peers descending on the capital for the pageantry, Buckingham Palace was turned into the most sophisticated ermine and coronet changing room the world has ever known.

My task was to prepare Lord Louis' robes, as I had done for the 1937 Coronation of King George VI and Queen Elizabeth.

His Lordship's robes, tunics, gold-laced trousers, boots and spurs had been stored in one of several air-tight tin boxes at Broadlands. When putting the clothes away, laying tissue paper along each fold, I had taken the precaution of scattering naphthalene crystals in the boxes against any possible invasion by moths.

I had not opened the Coronation robes boxes since the 1937 celebrations, but I found the garments were preserved like new and I hung them in the steam of a hot bath so that any minor crinkles would drop out.

Unfortunately, Lord Louis' robes needed fresh identification. Now an Earl and a member of the Order of the Garter, it was necessary from him to wear Royal blue and I had to have fresh robes made at Eade and Ravenscroft in the City. They were the specialists.

I paid £120 for the robes, but when I got back to the house Lord Louis had uncovered his father-in-law Lord Mount Temple's Coronation robes. Only a slight alteration to the ermine collar was needed and they fitted him perfectly.

'Dammit, Charles,' muttered Lord Louis thriftily, 'we've now got two sets of robes. Can't you take these new ones back?'

Hastily I returned to the City robemakers. My arrival was opportune. A late customer, on the verge of leaving the store empty handed, bought Lord Louis' robes for £170 – giving His Lordship a £50 profit on the transaction!

His Lordship was jubilant.

'Well done, Charles!' he beamed, 'you certainly know how to close a bargain. You would have made a fortune had I allowed you to work in Petticoat Lane!'

Everything was ready: tunics, robes, stars and neck decorations, ceremonial sword and holster, and His Lordship's cocked hat. Into Buckingham Palace's 'rugby scrum' we ventured with ermine tails flying. The place was very crowded and at Westminster Abbey we had the same problem. There we needed a changing annexe!

A remarkable coincidence occurred. Because of the pressure on space, I was asked if I would mind helping dress two other V.I.P. guests, a request I had similarly faced in 1937.

Imagine my surprise, and for that matter their surprise too, when I was landed with the same two 'customers' – the Duke of Gloucester and Sir Winston Churchill!

'I see we are all in the same team again, Charles!' mused Sir Winston, who suggested we might call for a tot of brandy before the proceedings began. A waiter brought a small brandy in a glass; I sent him back to get a bottle.

'Sir Winston won't look at a brandy that size,' I told him, recalling the Conservative leader's 1937 thirst, 'and please don't forget the soda.'

Sir Winston heard the conversation and smiled, lighting one of his famous cigars. 'Quite right, Charles,' he said, 'I don't know what this country is coming to.'

His Royal Highness the Duke of Gloucester and Lord Louis were happy to let Sir Winston hold court, the cigar fumes at least eliminating the aroma of naphthalene.

Lord Louis saved his brandy until the ceremony was over when he collected the family for some official Coronation photographs to be taken in Brick Street by Baron.

The Duke of Gloucester wasn't much of a tippler either and I think Sir Winston despaired of them both, for eyeing the brandy bottle, still half-full, he exclaimed, 'We didn't do it justice!'

I had met the Duke of Gloucester on several previous occasions. Once I delivered his full-dress uniform from St James's Palace to his country home in Aldershot in a last-minute attempt by Lord Louis to lure the Duke to a Naval function. But the Duke, who had spent the day on Army manoeuvres, wasn't having any of it.

'Will you please tell Lord Louis I can't make it,' the Duke told me. 'After the manoeuvres I'm too tired. Now be a good fellow and return my uniform to London where it belongs.'

Lord Louis was philosophical about my abortive mission.

'Well, at least we tried!' he said.

His Lordship was appointed personal A.D.C. to Her Majesty and this meant we travelled much more frequently to Windsor, Balmoral and Sandringham, as well as to Buckingham Palace.

I once stayed at Buckingham Palace in some style for ten days. My step-daughter Shirley slipped by one afternoon to see me and I was kindly delivered a tray of tea from the kitchen for my visitor. Having tea at Buckingham Palace was like a dream that had come true for Shirley. She asked if she could use the phone in my room to ring her boyfriend and her voice could not contain the thrill she was feeling.

'You'll never guess where I am phoning from,' she purred.

So much was happening at Buckingham Palace through this period. Lady Louis was due to go there for a State banquet when she discovered her tiara was missing. I was down in the country holding fort at Broadlands that day and a frantic call came from Her Ladyship's secretary, Elizabeth Ward, telephoning from the London house.

'Oh, Charles!' cried Miss Ward forlornly, 'we can't find Lady Louis' tiara anywhere. We've also lost two of her rings. The emerald one and the solitaire. We've turned the house upside down looking for them.'

She was understandably scared they had been stolen, but I knew the jewellery was safely with me at Broadlands. It wasn't that we had never considered the question of burglary. We had thoroughly gone into the possibility. Lord Louis once installed an electric beam burglary system, but it was totally inadequate as one didn't need to be an Indian fire-dancer to slither under the electric rays!

I demonstrated how it could be done by 'stealing' a cache of gems and His Lordship gasped, 'That's incredible, Charles. We'll have to get another bloody system.' A massive security programme was then undertaken.

As for Her Ladyship's 'missing' jewellery, I had stowed it in the main safe at Broadlands after its last use.

Louis on the steps at Broadlands playing with Juno's puppies

ss Margarita of Sweden, Lord Louis and the King of Sweden on the Portico steps at lands

site: Oona Chaplin removing her husband's hat and spectacles ready for my 8 m.m. cine camera.
and Lady Brabourne are on the left. They were on their way to plant saplings in the grounds at
lands, something Lord Louis always liked his guests to do, and I used to film the proceedings.
ie Chaplin gave an impromptu performance when he planted his (top). Lord Louis is on the left
roadlands' head gardener on the right. Above: Lord Louis with the Queen of Thailand who had
lanted a sapling

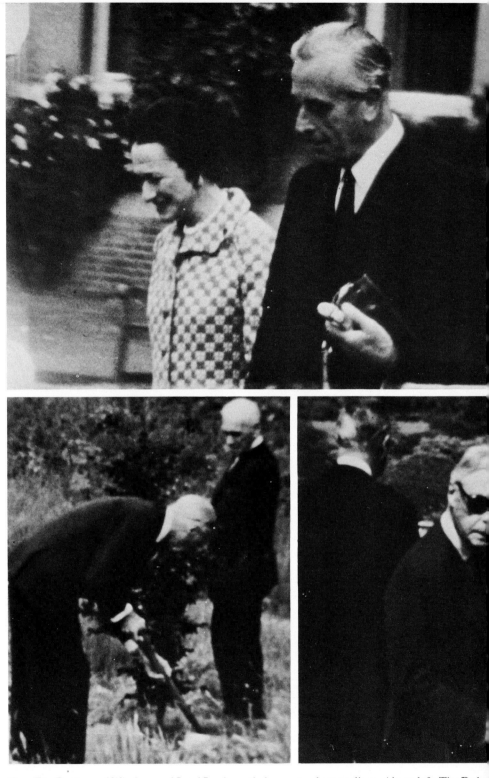

Top: The Duchess of Windsor and Lord Louis on their way to plant saplings. Above left: The Duke planting his. Above right: As the party left the planting the Duke of Windsor turned to give me a tip a him on my film with the money in his hands!

'Thank goodness it's there,' said Miss Ward, breathing with relief when I told her. 'Now the only problem we've got is getting it all to town in time.'

I glanced at my watch. It was 4.15 p.m.

'I'll put the lot on the train from Southampton,' I said. 'It's the only way we can get it there.'

'Isn't that chancy?' said Miss Ward.

'Not the way I plan to do it,' I assured her.

Of course it was a gamble, but I didn't want to alarm Miss Ward. I packed the tiara and rings into a sealed box, addressed them to Lord and Lady Louis, and drove to Southampton station. There I slapped a £5 note into the guard's hand, warning him not to take his eyes off the box until handing it over to His Lordship's runner, who would meet him at Waterloo.

I telephoned Miss Ward to give her the time of the train's arrival and asked her to inform me of the safe arrival of the box, which she duly did. Our little gamble had worked, thanks to the Southern Region guard's honesty. I hesitate to think what would have happened if he had chosen to disappear with the box en route. It could have been very embarrassing to have related such a story to Scotland Yard!

Her Ladyship was always very careful with her jewellery and she knew, like all women do with their possessions, every single piece.

When dressing for a cocktail party one evening she dropped a ring underneath the bed and left Violet, still acting as her maid, searching for it. Violet was wriggling right under the bed when she heard someone come into the room and a man's voice ask inquisitively, 'What's happening here?'

Violet's legs were protruding from under the bed and feeling in a helpless position she said, 'Her Ladyship has lost a ring on the floor and I'm looking for it.'

'Please let me help you,' offered the stranger, who bent down on the other side of the bed.

Poking his face forward into view, Violet recognized the caller. It was the King of Sweden!

'Oh, Your Majesty,' she said, so taken aback that her head hit the base of the bed, 'please don't worry, I will find it . . .'

'Why, here it is,' said the King, his fingers extracting the ring from the carpet pile where it had buried itself.

When Violet scrambled to her feet she curtsied and the King handed her the ring, a chuckle escaping his lips as he went on his way.

Many of Lord Louis' friends, other than those connected with the Navy or the monarchy, were in the entertainment profession. In later years he was to become known to many stars, including Frank Sinatra, Cary Grant and the delectable Shirley Maclaine. But even at this time Lord Louis could already claim quite a crop of friends in the film world.

Elizabeth Taylor came to Miss Pamela's 'coming out' ball dressed in a mermaid's sequined silver tail which rather caught His Lordship's nautical eye. Miss Taylor was then with Michael Wilding, soon to be her husband, and I must say she looked as exquisite in real life as she appeared on the screen.

Old friends Noël Coward and Charlie Chaplin, who would come with his wife Oona, rarely missed a party at Broadlands, and another familiar figure was Sir Malcolm Sargent, Britain's best known orchestral conductor, who would give impromptu piano recitals in the drawing room. Lord Louis' mother, who was prone to forget names, always referred to him as 'the bandleader'.

I can still hear her saying, 'Dickie, when is the bandleader coming down?'

11

The Death of
Lady Louis

Lord Louis achieved a lifelong ambition when he was appointed
First Sea Lord early in 1955. It was a position his father had once
occupied and both appointments, remarkably, had been made by Sir
Winston Churchill.

I had also been promoted, some months earlier, to the post of
butler when Frank Randall, after many years' service, retired to
Ireland.

I was then earning £12 a week and Violet was getting £6 for those
weeks she worked as maid. Considering our accommodation and
food were provided for us, we were not too badly off. And there were
always the odd perks. Besides, we were happy enough in making
ends meet. We needed no more. Our rewards were far greater in
merely serving Lord and Lady Louis. It was always an honour for us.
They were also very kind; we could always have turned to them for
help in any crisis.

I never considered that there was anything demeaning in being in
service; the application of a butler's duties required a certain art,
skill and patience. One also needed to be a diplomat, ready to say the
right thing at the proper time.

Lord Louis piled my plate high with work, but I didn't mind as long as I could always keep up with the backlog. I liked to be able to assure him that every job was in hand.

His Lordship thought we should live nearer to the main house when I became butler. In the stable yard was a tumble-down cottage, which I suggested we could move into. Lady Louis was horrified by the thought.

'Charles, it's in a terrible mess,' she said, 'it needs so much work done on it. Besides, do you really want to live in the stable yard?'

'Don't worry, Your Ladyship,' I said, 'it will do very nicely and I'll make it look a picture. You'll see.'

Violet and I worked for a year on the cottage in our off-duty hours. It needed major structural changes as well as a new staircase and flooring, but with the help of a carpenter and bricklayer, we at last got it ready, complete with built-in furniture and arched corridors. From being an empty shell it now resembled a home that one would have been happy to enter for the Ideal Home Exhibition, and we were very thrilled with it considering we only had limited 'do-it-yourself' experience.

Lord and Lady Louis could hardly believe their eyes at the transformation of their once-dilapidated cottage.

'Charles, it's just remarkable,' exclaimed Lord Louis, clearly staggered by the improvements. 'How on earth did you manage it all?'

Lady Louis said, 'I take back all I said, Charles. You've made this the smartest corner in the yard.'

His Lordship did not let it rest there. Not long after his visit he was on the telephone to us, saying, 'Look, Charles, we've got to show it off. I'm bringing Her Majesty and Prince Philip over to see it. Is that all right by you and Mrs Smith?'

'Yes, of course m'Lord,' I said.

Having Her Majesty and Prince Philip wend their way through the muddy stableyard to give Royal approval to our humble home was a tribute we could not have anticipated.

I said to Violet, who scurried round to ensure that everything was tidy, 'After this we will need to put a plaque up on the wall outside!'

We heard the Royal party arrive on the doorstep.

'You cannot really conceive what has happened here,' we heard Lord Louis saying. 'The place was falling to pieces and we might have had to gut it entirely if it hadn't been for Charles and his wife.'

Violet and I both greeted the Royal couple, who wanted to be shown right over the house. I explained to them how we came to design each room.

They were very impressed and the Queen said, 'You are going to be very happy here, I'm sure. It's absolutely lovely.'

Prince Philip joked, 'Perhaps we could hire your services, Charles. There are one or two odd jobs that we need doing at Buckingham Palace!'

Whenever Her Majesty and Prince Philip visited Broadlands it was typical of Lord Louis to devise some way by which the staff were made to feel part of the 'family'. Her Majesty once looked in on a servants' supper party and seeing the decoratively laid-out table turned to His Lordship and said, 'Dickie, why don't we eat down here instead? Charles has got it beautifully set.'

Indeed I had – and Lord Louis, scratching his head, realized how.

'Those candelabras,' said His Lordship gazing down on the table, 'haven't I seen them somewhere before, Charles?'

I shuffled uncomfortably on my feet.

'Yes, m'Lord,' I stammered, 'I was going to mention it to you, but I didn't think you would mind . . . they're yours!'

These particular candelabras were electrically lit and had been given to Lord Louis by his father. I thought I would borrow them for the occasion.

Fortunately, His Lordship saw the funny side of it and quipped, 'I take it you are going to send me the electricity bill as well!'

Her Majesty and Prince Philip's presence at Broadlands was much more frequent during the shooting season. The Queen's favourite Corgi dogs were never in evidence on these excursions, but instead she would bring down four gun dogs, two black and two golden Labradors.

Her Majesty would normally go out with the guns, but not until mid-morning. The shoot was always assembled at 9.15 with eight positions allotted by His Lordship with the aid of his cartridge placefinder. Even in bad weather the Queen enjoyed the shoot. She would wear a heavy drill mackintosh and headscarf and thickly lined boots and not worry how hard it might come to rain.

Most members of the shooting party would go on to Sir Thomas Sopwith's estate at Compton after their sweep through Broadlands, and Lord Louis would like to go with them. As host to the Queen, it was a bit of a tricky problem, but His Lordship would take the gamble and say, 'Charles, I'm leaving Her Majesty in your care!'

The Queen usually left Broadlands for Compton at a later hour or returned to Buckingham Palace. I would tuck a rug over her lap as she settled into her Rolls. I would then stand back on the drive and bow, and this little ceremony was usually watched by the household staff from the windows. Her Majesty would say, 'Thank you, Charles. I hope we will see you again soon.'

The Royal family was growing. The Queen and Prince Philip's second child, Princess Anne, was now an energetic five-year-old and judging by the way she scaled over the walls at Sandringham she promised to be quite a tomboy.

My first real 'audience' with Prince Charles took place in one of the corridors at Sandringham. He was now a lively boy of eight or nine. I was walking along the passage on my way to Lord Louis' room when the young Prince, in his school greys, ploughed headlong into me.

'Are you Charles?' he said, gazing up at me.

'Yes, Your Royal Highness. I am Charles,' I said.

'Super. You are just the fellow I've been told to see.'

'What about, Your Royal Highness?'

'Don't you keep a hamster at Broadlands? Well, I've got one too. Would you like to come and see it?'

Prince Charles led me along to his room. There, taking pride of place over the furnishings, was 'Hamster Castle', a model plaster-cast turreted mansion that had been built for his pet.

The young Prince clicked his fingers and the hamster peeped out through the doorway before gingerly emerging.

'There!' cried the Prince excitedly, 'I've taught it to do all sorts of things. Does your one do any tricks?'

'It isn't really mine, Your Royal Highness,' I said, 'it's Lord Louis', but I do look after it for him. As a matter of fact, we've made up an obstacle course he has to climb over if he wants to get a carrot to eat . . .'

The young Prince was enraptured by the thought.

'Maybe I can build one for mine too,' he said. 'That's a good idea.'

All around me a new generation had suddenly sprung. Lord and Lady Brabourne had another son Michael-John in 1950, Joanna was born in 1955, and two years later came Amanda. Broadlands was echoing to a lot of tiny feet! And I noticed an awful lot of carrycots and nappies!

There were other odd sights at Broadlands too. Society, as it had once been, was making its last stand in the fifties.

A golden Daimler glided on to the drive one day, the most ostentatious-looking car I had ever seen in my life, but which in the fifties became something of a hallmark for the much-publicized couple who owned it.

Out stepped Sir Bernard and Lady Docker, a couple intent on keeping society alive, but whose expeditions aboard their luxury yacht the *Shemara* often landed them in controversy.

They had been banned from Monaco by Prince Rainier after Lady Docker, in one of her notorious piques, had torn up a replica of the tiny principality's flag in a hotel restaurant. No doubt regarding Lord Louis as a 'fellow shipmate', they had made contact with him in the hope that he might act as mediator and help repair the rift. His Lordship was on close terms with Prince Rainier and Princess Grace.

While their chauffeur kept an almost regimental guard on the golden Daimler, the Dockers stayed on for lunch to press their side of the affair, but I could not see His Lordship getting involved in any way. He always made it a rule never to interfere in other people's squabbles.

I think in the end Sir Bernard and Lady Docker accepted His Lordship's neutrality, but they were still anxious to court the friendship of Broadlands. Every Christmas a six-foot basket of flowers would arrive for Her Ladyship from Lady Docker. It became increasingly embarrassing for Lady Louis to accept them.

She would shake her head and say, 'Oh, Charles, Lady Docker has done it again!'

16th July 1959

Dear Charles,

Commander Webb has sent us a copy of your accounts for the Garden Party at Broadlands from which we note that the total cost was only £376. 4s. 8d. which worked out at about 8s. 8d. per head. With any party of this nature, where the cost comes to below 10s 0d a head, is a very creditable effort on your part and Her Ladyship wishes to join me in commending you and thanking you for this result.

Next time, Her Ladyship would like to be consulted a little bit earlier about the menu but all went very well.

yours truly

Mountbatten of Burma

COCKTAIL PARTY BROADLANDS JULY 11th, 1959.

				£	s	d
Bottles	Whisky	@	32/4½	19	8	6
"	Gin	@	30/7½	101	1	3
"	Sherry	@	17/6	42	17	6
"	Noilly Prat	@	14/7	14	11	8
"	Martini	@	14/2	1	8	4
"	Rum	@	32/4	1	12	4
"	Orange Squash	@	3/-	3	12	0
Doz	Light Ale	@	17/-	7	13	0
"	Brown Ale	@	18/-	8	2	0
"	Larger	@	17/-	1	14	0
"	Ginger Beer	@	6/-		18	0
"	Bitter Lemon	@	7/-	1	1	0
1½s	Sausages	@	3/6	8	15	0
	Staff			6	10	0
	Lowmans Acc			157	0	0
			£	376	4	8

At least old and needy folk in Romsey would benefit, as would the hospitals, because there were so many flowers that Lady Louis couldn't keep them all.

Her Ladyship liked to see fresh flowers always in the house, but when it was left for me to arrange them, I tended to mix blooms and colours in the same vase. That wasn't to Her Ladyship's liking.

'Charles,' she corrected me, 'don't go on mixing up the flowers like that. They lose their whole effect. Please keep the same blooms and colours together.'

Her Ladyship had her little set ways and was perhaps more sensitive than Lord Louis. She liked to know what was going on in the household all the time and if it ever appeared that I had crossed her authority then she would not hesitate to admonish me.

I once helped a new cook who was too nervous to make out the weekly menus by doing them myself, and Her Ladyship said sharply, 'Why is she nervous? She has no reason to be. You must tell her how the menus are done, Charles, and make sure she does them herself.'

When arranging a garden party in the grounds I was again in trouble over the wretched menu. His Lordship wrote me a note of thanks but saved the last paragraph to tick me off for not consulting Her Ladyship earlier about the food I had chosen. My feeling was that Her Ladyship placed too much unnecessary strain on herself. She worried about too many domestic things from which I could have relieved the pressure.

She was involved with so many more important matters. She was a workaholic. So many causes, so many activities, were important to her. She would edge perilously towards exhaustion, but would conceal it. She also suffered terribly from neuralgia.

Through one spell when she wasn't feeling so well, her Sealyham dog Mizzen also became sick.

'I'm afraid we're both a couple of crocks this morning, Charles,' said Her Ladyship when I took some orange juice up to her bedroom. 'I don't know what has got into us.'

I looked at Her Ladyship. She was awfully pallid.

'Don't you think, Your Ladyship, we should call the doctor?' I suggested.

When Lady Louis agreed, I realized she was going through more pain than she cared to say.

Not wishing to allow her dog to suffer while she received attention, she added, 'I think you had also better call the vet to have a look at Mizzen.'

Her Ladyship gave me the names and numbers to call and I fixed appointments for later that morning. At 11.00 a.m. the first caller arrived. Standing in the hall was an elegantly dressed gentleman in a pinstripe suit.

I had no hesitation in concluding that he was the doctor, as my past knowledge of vets led me to believe that they all lived in baggy tweeds.

'Good morning, Sir,' I said, 'I will take you upstairs to see Lady Louis.'

At Her Ladyship's bedroom I announced the doctor's arrival, but Lady Louis leaned from her pillow in surprise.

'Oh, Charles, you've got it all wrong. This is Mr Gould the veterinary surgeon. I'm sure he's come to see Mizzen!'

I gulped with embarrassment.

Some days later His Lordship was feeling a bit under the weather. Lady Louis told him not to worry. 'Leave it to Charles, darling. He'll get the vet for you!'

At the turn of the year Her Ladyship was back in good spirit and health and there was a golden start to 1960 for the family.

Miss Pamela was to be a bride. The bridegroom was Mr David Hicks, one of London's most fashionable interior designers. We all approved. Mr Hicks, who had been a familiar figure at Broadlands for some time, was courteous and charming. We all thought, among the staff, that he would make a very good husband for Pamela.

It was indeed a white wedding. Snow fell heavily in Romsey overnight, providing the most romantic setting for the occasion, with the Royal family attending and Princess Anne as a bridesmaid.

The reception was organized at Broadlands and I ordered a beautiful wedding cake for the couple which was a replica of the house itself. It was so perfect in scale that Miss Pamela and her husband hesitated before cutting it!

As butler in charge, I tried to make allowance for every kind of eventuality and with sporadic power cuts occurring I stored a reserve of candles and laid claim on some forty silver candlesticks from the family collection. It was just as well. At the very height of the reception the banqueting room was plunged into darkness by a power failure, but before any panic descended I marshalled the staff into the hall with the candles all lit. The effect was infinitely more intimate than before the power cut.

Lady Pamela and Mr Hicks left for their honeymoon and four days later Lady Louis set off on a tour of the Far East on behalf of the St John Ambulance Brigade and Save the Children fund. Suddenly, after all the activity, the house seemed strangely empty.

News of Lady Louis' progress in the Far East was scattered, but we knew she had reached Borneo safely and all seemed to be going well. We were hardly prepared for the shock that was to come.

Lord Louis was in London and I had taken the day off to play a game of golf with my cousin Tommy Swailes at Chippenham. For

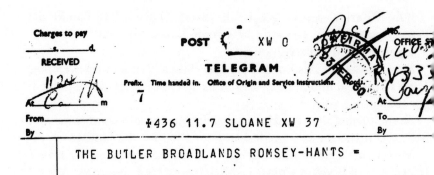

THE BUTLER BROADLANDS ROMSEY-HANTS =

PLEASE THANK ALL THOSE MEMBERS OF THE STAFF WH

JOINED IN SENDING THE MOST CHARMING MESSAGE WHI

I HAVE RECEIVED SINCE OUR TERRIBLE LOSS AND WHI

HAS COMFORTED ME GREATLY = MOUNTBATTEN OF BURM

some reason I was ill at ease and I played a lousy game. When I go
to the clubhouse, one of the members, his face showing concern
came over to me and asked if I had heard about Lady Louis.

'No,' I said, 'what's happened?'

'There was a news flash on the radio that she has died in Borneo,
he said.

It was difficult to believe. I telephoned Commander Ben Webb
Lord Louis' secretary, who confirmed the sad news.

I drove back immediately to Broadlands, knowing that Lord
Louis would return there as soon as he could and realizing how
desperate and heartbroken he would be. From Broadlands I sen
him a cable on behalf of the staff expressing our deep sorrow.

Slowly we learned the extent of the punishing demands that Lady
Louis had made on herself. The heavy schedule for the tour, th
burden of her causes and charitable work, had finally taken their toll

If there was any consolation at all it was that thankfully her death had not been a lingering one. She had passed away peacefully in her sleep.

The world mourned her loss and special Post Office deliveries were made almost hourly to the house conveying more than 6,000 telegrams and letters from near and far. This moving expression of grief and sorrow poured in from kings and queens, presidents, premiers, and friends in high places, but the majority of the communications came from ordinary people who had come to love Lady Louis and her unselfish dedication to life. Tributes came from soldiers and refugees in distant lands, from Burma and India particularly, from people who perhaps owed their lives to Her Ladyship's devotion.

At Broadlands, in the drawing room, with one of these telegrams crumpled between his trembling hands, I found Lord Louis, tears flowing from his eyes.

I put a comforting hand on his shoulder and whispered to him, 'My Lord, we all loved Lady Louis too. All our thoughts are with you.'

He turned and dabbed his face dry with his handkerchief.

'Thank you, Charles,' he said.

Lady Louis' body was flown back to England and laid in Romsey Abbey, where only six weeks before we had seen Her Ladyship so joyful at Miss Pamela's wedding.

It was decided that the members of the estate staff should keep vigil over Lady Louis' coffin and I stood guard for the last three hours before the funeral journey.

Lady Louis had requested that she should be buried at sea. The First Sea Lord offered the frigate H.M.S. *Wakeful* and attended the funeral himself, together with Prince Philip in his Admiral's uniform and his mother, Princess Alice of Greece, among the family mourners.

An Indian frigate, the *Trishul*, also acted as escort when the H.M.S. *Wakeful* left Portsmouth for the open sea with Lady Louis' coffin on board.

When the funeral cortège left Romsey Abbey for Portsmouth, I took out Lady Louis' other white Sealyham dog Snippie to catch a

BROADLANDS,
ROMSEY,
HAMPSHIRE.

TELEPHONE
ROMSEY 3333.

25th February 1960.

Dear Charles,

I want to express to you
my heart-felt thanks for having
been one of those who stood watch
in the Abbey so that my wife was
not alone throughout her last night
in Romsey.

yours sincerely

Mountbatten of Burma

8th July 1960

Dear Charles,

I would like you and Mrs. Smith to have a souvenir of Lady Louis and so am sending you one of the last photographs taken in her lifetime at Singapore in February talking to the child of one of our Gurkha soldiers in hospital.

It is framed in one of her own frames.

Yours sincerely

Mountbatten of Burma

22nd April 1961

Dear Charles

I felt you would like to
have a copy of this pictorial
record of Lady Louis' life to
remind you of your long
association with her.

*It is for Mrs. Smith,
too, of course*

yours sincerely

Mountbatten of Burma

Above: Lord Louis at Broadlands with Pancho, 'the greatest friend and companion I have ever known among dogs'

Right: With Violet outside the Mountbattens' Wilton Crescent house in London before we went to Buckingham Palace to attend a Garden Party

Lord Louis signed and gave me the portrait of himself. He gave me three portraits like this, all of
showing him dressed for a State occasion when I had been responsible for his robing. Prince Cl
signed and gave me the picture of himself for Christmas, and he gave Violet the teak trinket box i
with his crest in silver. Queen Louise of Sweden gave me the floral ashtray inlaid with silver and i
will she left me the patterned trinket box. Lord Louis presented me with the Viceroy of India me
has my name inscribed on the back. He also gave me the gold cufflinks and the Chinese mode
pagoda. He gave Violet the gold bracelet

glimpse of the final departure of his mistress and the dog's instincts seemed to tell him what was happening. He stayed woefully in my arms and whimpered sadly.

'That was a very touching gesture, Charles. It was kind of you, and Her Ladyship would have appreciated it,' said Lord Louis later.

It was hard to contain my own tears. I had started with the Mountbattens as Lady Louis' footman and I had travelled with her to many foreign parts.

Before she left for Borneo she had asked me to have all the consul and writing tables in the house restored in her absence and to get the settees and chairs in the saloon recovered. All this work was put in hand, but she did not live to see it completed.

She telephoned me only twenty-four hours before catching her plane. I was out and she spoke to my wife who passed on Her Ladyship's message to me. She wanted some extra sweaters and woolies for her travels and she asked for them to be put on the train to London so that she could pack them to go away with.

Her Ladyship told my wife, 'Please look after Charles while I'm away, Mrs Smith, because he's inclined to overtax himself. He really should have a good rest.'

Grey, bleak days enshrouded Broadlands. The house was silent and still. Servants talked in hushed voices.

In Lady Louis' room I noticed in a small green vase on her writing table the sprig of white heather I had found at Balmoral and given to Her Ladyship seven years before. She had kept it all that time.

We were to miss Her Ladyship deeply; we all had to find ways of re-adapting ourselves, but it wasn't easy. Our task was to comfort Lord Louis in every way possible.

Some weeks later a film of Lady Louis' tour of the Far East arrived at Broadlands and I watched it with Lord Louis. On the screen we saw Lady Louis inspecting a St John Ambulance parade just prior to her arrival in Borneo, and His Lordship remarked, 'Charles, just look at Her Ladyship there. She looks absolutely worn out.'

When the film was over, his cheeks were tear-stained.

'She worked herself much too hard, Charles,' he said, 'she didn't know when to stop.'

Lady Patricia gave Violet one or two of Lady Louis' ceremonial

Bought by Father Christmas and
returned to the original owner.
The family were deeply touched
by the generous gesture by which
these plates were sold on the
occasion of the auction for the
benefit of the Edwina Mountbatten
Homes.

These were two plates I gave
to be sold at the above auction
Lord Louis bought them for £22 -.
and gave them back to me at
christmass

Charles Smith

dresses, which she proudly preserves today. Lady Pamela also gave Violet a pair of Her Ladyship's gold-coloured evening dress shoes. I received a bequest of £700.

His Lordship came to rely on me almost totally on the running of the house after Her Ladyship's passing. I took charge of the cleaning of the house, the regular renovation of the soft furnishings, the daily catering and the ordering of supplies, all the things that Lady Louis had been responsible for in the past.

For some reason His Lordship drifted out of his study to work and he would take his papers through into the drawing room and use a writing desk there. One could detect the loneliness that had crept over him. His face and his thoughts were sombre.

Ironically, it was another crisis which rallied Lord Louis from the depths of mourning. Broadlands was struck with a wave of dry rot that threatened the whole house. His Lordship, regarding it as a challenge, rose to save his house in the way he had strived to save his ship from destruction. He ordered a massive reconstruction programme that was to cost hundreds of thousands of pounds.

Most of the rooms had to be stripped right back and some precious ornamental decorations were lost, although the priceless gold-embossed ceilings and walls of the saloon were miraculously preserved. The restoration work took three years and a lot of changes were made.

We anticipated that Lord Louis might wish to shut off Her Ladyship's room from further use, but we were grossly mistaken.

'Her Ladyship would not like that to happen and neither would I,' directed Lord Louis. 'We will go on using the room for our guests.'

When each room had been freshly plastered and decorated, it was necessary to replace curtains and carpets, and when it came to the renovation of Her Majesty's room – the Portico Room – His Lordship asked me to get a set of patterns from Sanderson's.

I stumbled on a beautiful chintz pattern that incorporated line drawings of the profile of the young Queen Victoria and her Prince Consort that had originally been designed for the Royal yacht, the *Victoria and Albert*, in 1854.

I knew that this would be the pattern that Lord Louis would choose, but I didn't want to make it appear that I had made the decision for him, so I took back to Broadlands four or five alternative designs so that he could make the final selection.

His Lordship instantly picked out the chintz and said, 'Charles, what do you think of this one?'

'Yes, m'Lord,' I said, 'I think this is a good one, and what's more it is very economical. We need 200 yards and Sanderson's say that buying it in bulk we can get it for £2 a yard.'

When the curtains, canopy and other furnishings were co-ordinated with the same chintz the Portico Room was breathtaking, and Her Majesty and Prince Philip were overjoyed with the transformation when they saw it.

Work still continued at the rear of the house, and when Lord Louis had to go overseas I took it upon myself to order the decorations for a guest's closet. I did so as a matter of expediency as the architect and decorators were ready to proceed and guests were due shortly. I chose a pastel green, and had the toilet, bidet and a pair of hand basins installed in a matching colour.

When Lord Louis got back I sensed he wasn't too pleased. I heard his voice boom through the house.

'Charles,' he roared, 'who gave orders for this closet to be done like this?'

'I did, my Lord,' I said.

'But, Charles, you know very well that I like to make these kind of decisions myself.'

'Yes, m'Lord,' I agreed, 'but you've got six guests coming down this weekend and the closet would have been out of use otherwise.'

'I see,' said Lord Louis, stroking his chin. 'Very well, Charles, but in future please contact me before going ahead with things like this.'

Two days later I heard Lord Louis summoning me from the rear of the house and I found him inspecting the closet once more. My heart sank. I was sure that he was going to put me through the mill again. But no.

'Maybe, Charles, I was a bit hasty,' he said. 'I've given it some thought, but I can't think of any design I would have chosen in preference to yours. I must be honest and tell you that I like the way it has been done.'

There were so many alterations going on in the house that even I became confused, and when our weekend guests arrived I committed what Lord Louis later described as a 'glorious clanger' when I walked into a bathroom that had once been a dressing room.

Sitting in the bath, in all her glory, was the very beautiful Lady Anastasia 'Zia' Wernher, the wife of Sir Harold Wernher, the millionaire businessman.

Lady Anastasia threw me the blankest of stares, while I began to mumble, 'I beg your pardon, ma'am. Your husband is dressing and he sent me for his grey suit. This used to be the dressing room . . .'

Turning my eyes from Her Ladyship's direction, I backed awkwardly out of the door still muttering apologies.

My face beetroot-coloured, I thought it prudent to make my confession to Sir Harold. He was tickled pink.

'Well, if my wife will sit in the tub without locking the door what can she expect!' he laughed.

At dinner that night Lord Louis introduced me to Lady Zia.

'This is Charles,' said Lord Louis to our guest, 'I don't know whether you've had the opportunity of meeting . . .'

Her Ladyship beamed.

'Yes. We met in my bathroom this morning, didn't we, Charles?' she said.

12

Charles – Butler or Prince?

'Charles!' Lord Louis' unmistakable command echoed through the corridors of the house and I quickened my step.

Coming from another direction, assuming that he had been the one to be summoned, was Prince Charles, our house guest. We practically collided at Lord Louis' door.

'Which one of us does he want?' the young Prince asked.

'I really don't know, Sir,' I replied. 'Shall we go through and find out?'

An expression of bemusement descended on Lord Louis' face as we followed one another into the room.

'Oh, I see,' exclaimed His Lordship, 'I've caught you both.'

He looked at Prince Charles and apologized. 'I'm sorry, Your Royal Highness, but it's Charles I actually want to have a word with.'

His Lordship had called me to thrash out the travel arrangements for a tour he was to make, but this wasn't the only incident where confusion was to arise between Prince Charles and myself. Bearing the same christian name always seemed to land us in a muddle.

On a later occasion, His Lordship's cry again brought us both to his room.

'Oh, not again!' Lord Louis cried in exasperation. This time his business was with the Prince.

It didn't stop there. Even when Her Majesty and other guests at Broadlands dinner parties mentioned 'Charles' we would both instinctively respond.

In the end Prince Charles came up with a solution.

'One of us has to change his name,' he said.

'Well, Your Royal Highness,' I said, 'I don't think Her Majesty or *Burke's Peerage* would allow you to do that, so it had better be me, but I refuse to be known as "Charlie". I hate the name.'

'So do I,' nodded the Prince, 'it gets tiring when people keep calling you a "proper Charlie". I've experienced it myself, Charles, so I know precisely what you mean!'

I paused.

'Of course,' I said, 'my family call me "Pip" – my middle name happens to be Paxton – and that's a nickname I have no objection to.'

'Pip? No, there's nothing wrong with that,' said the Prince. 'Let's see how it works out.'

Unfortunately, Pip didn't catch on at all. The name 'Charles' was too much ingrained on the household and Lord Louis concluded that it was as elegant for a butler to have the name as it was for a Prince!

Oddly enough, the 'identity crisis' that persisted in the household was when callers mistook my voice on the telephone for Lord Louis'. There was no conscious attempt on my part to impersonate His Lordship, but over the years and without realizing it my voice had developed similar aristocratic tones! Even my wife found it difficult to distinguish between us on the telephone.

She was not alone. I would take calls from Lady Patricia and Lady Pamela, who would chirp up, 'Hello, Daddy . . .' before I could correct them. Close friends would come on stronger, 'Hello, Dickie darling . . .' only to fall silent when they found they were chatting up the butler!

I could not always cut in and tell callers of their error until the first burst of conversation was exhausted. Once I listened to the King of

Sweden running on at length about an Italian archaeological trip he had just made.

'Dickie,' he said, 'you really should have been with us!'

At that stage, as the King took fresh breath, I was able to interject, 'I'm sorry, Your Majesty, and I am glad you had a rewarding trip, but this is Charles the butler!'

His Majesty's conversation stumbled, but then he chortled, 'Well, you should have come too, Charles!'

I would take the majority of the calls in the house as a routine 'screening' procedure, while others would be dealt with by Lord Louis' secretary when on duty at Broadlands.

If Her Majesty telephoned from Buckingham Palace there would be less likelihood of confusion as a secretary would first enquire whether His Lordship was present.

Lord Louis' affectionate name for the Queen was 'Lilibet', but it was only used in personal conversations. On all other occasions, especially public functions, His Lordship would address the Queen as 'Your Majesty'.

When Her Majesty was staying at Broadlands, there was one matter of State that was never left unattended. The Queen's daily despatch box, containing confidential papers from her Prime Minister and Cabinet, was a mission of vital importance. Every afternoon the red leather-faced box, with the Sovereign's crest on its lid, would be delivered by two postmen who would make the special journey from London by van. The box would be in a mail bag, the neck of which was chained and padlocked. I would sign for it on its safe delivery and then remove the despatch box from the bag by opening the padlock with a key entrusted to me by a Palace detective.

The box itself was also locked and the key to it was held by the Queen, who would open it after I had conveyed it to her in the Chinese Room, where she would use a writing desk to sift through all the papers that had been sent to her.

I was always a little apprehensive about the despatch box if Her Majesty was out when it arrived. But she calmed my anxieties.

'Don't worry, Charles,' she said, 'just put the despatch box in my room. It will be safe enough there until I return.'

Normally the Queen would take one or two hours to deal with all the papers and correspondence. When she had finished she would ring me and I would place the box back inside its mail bag, lock it, and await its collection by the two postmen.

This was the one and only 'official' duty that I was aware Her Majesty undertook at Broadlands. It was always my guess that the Queen and Prince Philip came to Romsey to escape the rigours and pressures of the monarchy. It was clearly a rest for them both. There was no one there to harass them, no pomp and protocol to observe.

As a token of honour, Her Majesty would occupy the head of the table at meal times and Lord Louis, forsaking what would normally be his seat, would sit on the Queen's right and face Prince Philip across the table.

On rainy days the Queen would spend her leisure time doing a jigsaw puzzle, a hobby that was quite a favourite occupation at Broadlands with all members of the Royal family. Searching for lost, dropped pieces on the floor would sometimes entail my help − especially when the very last piece was agonizingly missing!

The Queen's soft spot for Lord Louis was evident when she presented him with a Labrador dog that came to be named Pancho. I would take Pancho out for long walks and he would usually accompany me when I went out for a round of golf, knowing my plans when I changed into a pair of plus fours.

One day I had got all ready to go out to play when Lord Louis summoned me.

'M'Lord,' I said, 'I'm in my golfing togs.'

'That doesn't matter. You don't have to dress specially for me,' His Lordship said.

'But, Your Lordship,' I argued, 'Pancho is waiting for me to take him out and now I'm in my plus fours I would never be forgiven . . .'

His Lordship meditated for a moment.

'Oh very well, Charles. Only you would dream of putting a dog before its master!' he said resignedly.

Her Majesty would also send Lord Louis the occasional pair of grouse, knowing His Lordship's taste for them. They would usually come when His Lordship had missed a shoot at Sandringham or Balmoral.

There was plenty of shooting, of course, at Broadlands but the

4/6/72

Dear Charles,

I hope you found the tiny key holded in a small mauve with a clip in the top drawer of the table between my bed and the window or posted it. I've got the instructions re Jeeves — thank you

We bought the jig-saw puzzles for Ireland. Can you please order 2 boxes. It might be best to get Lady Pamela to pick them up & bring them out on 12th.

Alternatively it might be simple to have them posted here.

Fortunately we have one old puzzle to get on with.

I hope all is well

Yours sincerely

Mountbatten of Burma

Will you have a word with John Barratt about a young man to help your staff over the shooting here say 20th October to after Xmas.

MB

catch varied from season to season, as it did on all estates. His Lordship once unloaded two barrels when he sighted what he thought was a fox. Instead, the victim was a well known socialite who was following the shoot dressed in a foxtail wrap which trailed conspicuously down her back.

'Silly damn woman!' roared Lord Louis when he discovered the mistake he had made.

Luckily the woman was not badly hurt and the one or two pellets that penetrated her thick clothing were removed from her seat at Romsey hospital.

The Queen's love of horses was shared by Lord Louis, but he was never very interested in going to the races, although he once ran in one in Malta, wearing red and white silks. He actually romped ahead of the field to win first prize!

I remember getting him all dressed up in a grey topper and tails for Royal Ascot, only to have a last-minute telephone call bring about the cancellation of his plans.

'Charles,' he said, with the suggestion of relief in his voice, 'I've got to go to the Admiralty. It's very important.'

His Lordship lived up to his popular image as the avuncular figure within the Royal family. The Queen and Prince Philip never hesitated to consult him, drawing on his vast wisdom, logic and experience. He was on speaking terms with so many world leaders; he could talk with authority on a diversity of complex situations.

The influence of Lord Louis on Prince Charles was more telling, and when the Prince becomes King Lord Louis' influence will, I am sure, stand him in good stead. For he aimed Prince Charles in the way he channelled Prince Philip, with Gordonstoun, polo and the Navy being part of the course.

It was at Broadlands that I saw just how much Prince Charles admired Lord Louis. There are questions a boy doesn't like asking his father. They were easy to ask of a great uncle like Lord Louis. Uncle Dickie always had the answer!

When the Prince dropped by on Broadlands unannounced, His Lordship would always be delighted to see him. In spite of the generations between them, they were like two old pals. Prince Charles usually stayed two or three days at a time and he would occupy one of the smaller bedrooms on the second floor. He would go out riding with Lord Louis and they would practise polo together.

Prince Charles is so natural in every way and I think Lord Louis, by example, passed on to him the secret of being able to adapt an easy-going frame of mind, enabling him to communicate with people in all walks of life. Strolling about on the estate the Prince would pass the time of day with anyone he bumped into. His kindness and cordiality were always apparent.

When I was sent to Portsmouth to pick up some things for Lord Louis from aboard the Royal yacht *Britannia* it was His Royal Highness who greeted me on deck.

'This must be your first visit, Charles,' he said. 'Come, I will show you over.'

The *Britannia* is even more luxurious than its predecessor the *Victoria and Albert*, with spacious, streamlined cabins and saloons, and its bridge carrying the most up-to-date navigational equipment and devices. Prince Charles impressed on me the directions along the gangways, ensuring that I would not lose my bearings on future visits.

I valued greatly the trust that Prince Charles placed in me and through the years our friendship grew.

When Prince Charles invited Violet and myself to a garden party at Buckingham Palace, it was a very special honour. When we were formally presented to Her Majesty she whispered to me, 'This time, Charles, we're arranging the tea!'

It was quite a day for us — Violet investing in a new smart costume and hat, while I hired a grey topper and tails from Moss Brothers,

'Now you know how uncomfortable it feels!' Lord Louis commented.

When we left Romsey the skies threatened rain and Violet took a mackintosh with her. But when we reached London the sun was shining brightly. I dropped the raincoat off at the Buckingham Palace west gate where a page, whom I knew from past visits, kindly offered to look after it.

When, after the garden party, I went to retrieve it a policeman apprehended me.

'And where might you be going, Sir?' he enquired.

Charles.

A very happy Xmas —

Charles.

The Lord Chamberlain is
commanded by Her Majesty to invite

Mr and Mrs Charles Smith
to a Thanksgiving Service on the occasion of
the Twenty-Fifth Anniversary of the Marriage of
The Queen and The Duke of Edinburgh
in Westminster Abbey
on Monday, 20th November, 1972 at 11.0 a.m.

Morning Dress
or Lounge Suit

An answer is requested to
The Lord Chamberlain,
St. James's Palace, London, S.W.1.

I am sure it was an officer I had seen before on duty outside Buckingham Palace, but in my topper and tails he did not recognize me – until the page came out and rescued me!

Prince Charles also remembered us at Christmas. He sent Violet a teak trinket box inlaid with his crest in silver, and I received a signed portrait of His Royal Highness which still holds prime position on our sideboard.

In 1972 we were again honoured when the Queen invited us to the service in Westminster Abbey to celebrate her silver wedding anniversary.

When all the repairs and renovations to Broadlands were complete, Lord Louis suggested that I should go for a three-week holiday with Violet to his favourite summer retreat, his home in Ireland, the turreted Classiebawn Castle with its panoramic views across the sea.

Even after Her Ladyship's death, Lord Louis continued with tradition and he would arrange the family's summer holiday there, usually during the month of August.

Now, in September, he was offering the house and all the facilities that went with it to my wife and myself.

'Use my rooms, don't move into any other quarters,' insisted Lord Louis. 'I want you both to be as comfortable as possible. You will find Ireland is very beautiful at this time of year.'

Classiebawn was manned by a skeleton staff employed by Lord Louis. Mr Paddy O'Grady was the butler and his wife acted as housekeeper, while the general administration was undertaken by Miss Gorebooth.

We had a marvellous holiday and as for sightseeing, one had merely to sit on Lord Louis' loo to take in a glorious view across the Atlantic!

Lord Louis' rooms were elegant, and it was difficult for us not to feel out of place when occupying them! Indeed, we were so conscious of this that we found it was impossible for us to take our meals in the main dining room. It was completely out of character. We could not accept the idea of Mr and Mrs O'Grady waiting on us, so we would sit, much more happily, at the kitchen table and have our meals with them.

His Lordship's consideration for our well-being was beyond measure. When he missed our silver wedding anniversary (and I absorbed his wrath for not reminding him), he offered us the use of his new London house in Kinnerton Street for a weekend as well as providing theatre tickets and arranging a restaurant dinner to follow. Alternatively, we could have thrown a party for our family and friends at Broadlands. But a weekend in London attracted us more.

On these occasions, Lord Louis would make every single arrangement for us, as he demonstrated when, in earlier years, he sent through a pair of tickets for the gala opening of Noël Coward's new musical *Sail Away* at the Savoy Theatre which had been transformed to resemble the deck of a battleship. There were so many gestures like these.

When my wife developed arthritis, His Lordship persuaded Violet to go to a Harley Street specialist and have treatment at his expense.

At Christmas, ordering gold bracelets for his grandchildren, he discovered he had purchased one too many.

'What shall I do with it, Charles?' he said, thinking aloud. 'I know. Do you think Mrs Smith would like it?'

He was very fond of Violet. Driving through London and close to the house where she was born, Lord Louis turned to me and said, 'Charles, you had better raise your hat.'

We were very fortunate.

His Lordship would also give us many presents for our home: pieces of porcelain or pictures to hang on the walls, including a signed print of his beloved H.M.S. *Kelly* painted by Montague Dawson.

Lady Patricia and Lady Pamela would also shower us with many treasured presents, and Lord Louis' sister, Queen Louise of Sweden, would always bring me a tie whenever she came to Broadlands.

'That's one less for my husband, Charles,' she would say. 'I'm afraid the King has got hundreds and he doesn't know what to do with them all!'

Queen Louise also knew of my love for antiques and porcelain and she once gave me a lovely floral ceramic ashtray inlaid with silver. When she died in 1965 she left me a miniature trinket box – one from

9th January '70

Dear Mrs. Smith,

I am writing to give
you & Charles my best wishes on
the occasion of your silver wedding.
Several months ago Charles told
me of this great event but I failed
to make a written note & my memory
without note is quite hopeless.

Unfortunately Charles did not
remind me of the date at all — so I am

...after I forgot all about it. I'm so sorry.

As a Silver Wedding Present I would like to offer Charles & you the use of my house — 2 Kinnerton St — while I am away in the Royal Yacht for a spree in London.

I'd also like to give you tickets to a theatre & a dinner at a restaurant of your choice in London to celebrate our silver wedding.

Or if you prefer to have your family here for a celebration I'll give you a dinner for them in the house — whichever you best prefer — Yours sincerely

Mountbatten of Burma

14th June 1962

Dear Charles,

I am sending you herewith two seats in row 'F' for the Gala Performance of Noël Coward's "Sail Away" at the Savoy Theatre on 28th June.

You and your wife can have my old room to spend the night at 2 Wilton Crescent.

I shall be going down to Broadlands on Friday 29th but the rest of the weekend party are not expected until the morning of Saturday, 30th.

I am leaving three seats in row 'E' for three of the Wilton Crescent household.

Yours sincerely

Mountbatten of Burma

her own collection – which the widowed King brought especially to Broadlands for me.

'The Queen wanted you to have this, Charles, and she left it for you in her will,' he said, summoning me to his room.

King Gustaf continued to come to Broadlands until he, too, sadly passed away in 1973. They were greatly missed.

13

The Loneliness of Lord Louis

Time is said to be a great healer, but in the passing years I knew that Lord Louis experienced moments of acute loneliness. The memory and love of Her Ladyship had not diminished.

When he was alone at home, without friends or family around him, he would take his dinner into the television room.

Comedy shows and soap operas weren't exactly His Lordship's cup of tea. His mentality couldn't cope with them; he was concerned about world events and programmes like *Panorama*, *World in Action* and *Horizon* were much more his preference.

Lord Louis' only companion in the room would be his Labrador Pancho, the dog the Queen had given him, who would sprawl out at his feet on the carpet. His Lordship loved the dog greatly and he was filled with distress when Pancho died suddenly from liver cancer. Lord Louis was in New York at the time and I called three veterinary surgeons in a vain attempt to save Pancho.

Shocked by the news in New York, His Lordship wrote to me: 'I share with you and Mrs Smith the loss of the greatest friend and companion I have ever known among dogs. He was unique. I am grateful to you both for the loving attention you gave him in his

BROADLANDS.
ROMSEY.
HAMPSHIRE.

TELEPHONE
ROMSEY 3333.

In New York

19th March 1968

My dear Charles,

I have just heard the tragic news that
Pancho had to be put down after he was found to
have cancer of the liver.

I share with you and Mrs. Smith the loss of
the greatest friend and companion I have ever
known among dogs. He was unique. I am grateful to
you both for the loving attention you gave him
in his last illness and I can imagine what an
agonising experience it was.

I can hardly bear to think of Broadlands
without him. He was such a companion.

Lady Patricia tells me she arranged with you
to get on to Meldrum, the Dog Keeper at Sandringham,
to get his son Kelly sent down as soon as possible
to Broadlands. Perhaps Ron Heath or Robert could
drive up in my Ford and collect him direct from
Sandringham or from Liverpool Street Station if
he can be sent down by train.

Please arrange with Grass that one of the
Keepers, preferably the one living in the
Stafferton's house to take him in for house training
as it would be much too much to ask you to do this.

I am keen to have him house trained as soon
as possible so that I may have some companionship
when I get back on 6th April.

yours sincerely,

Mountbatten of Burma

S. I've just decided to send a telegram to confirm with
to ensure Kelly is brought down quick.

last illness and I can imagine what an agonizing experience it was.'

Pancho's son Kelly was immediately brought to Broadlands from the Sandringham kennels so that Lord Louis would have some companionship about the house when he returned from America.

Kelly and his master became instant friends, but there was still something missing in His Lordship's life that nothing could fill. Some people would ask me if I thought His Lordship would ever marry again and my answer was always the same.

'I am sure he won't,' I would say. 'I don't think the question has so much as crossed his mind.'

His Lordship enjoyed the company of women. It was rejuvenating for him. His own personality and wit would sparkle in female presence and his spirits would always be lifted when Her Majesty was at Broadlands.

The Duchess of Windsor was said to find Lord Louis a bit of a bore, but she gave no indication of that on her visits to Broadlands, where she was only too pleased to be asked to plant a copper beech tree on the estate. His Lordship, glancing at the former Mrs Simpson, ruminated, 'She is a remarkable looking woman for her age, Charles. I don't know how she manages to stay as slim as she does.'

I filmed the Duchess that day with the Duke, and while I was doing so the Duke extracted £2 from his trouser pocket, whereupon Lord Louis exclaimed, 'Don't miss this shot, Charles. His Royal Highness is sorting out your tip!'

Many socialite beauties visited Broadlands for the various house parties, but I don't think any made enough impression on His Lordship for him to consider pursuing a fresh romantic attachment. Etched on his heart were the memories of Edwina and they meant too much to him. Inevitably, he would make comparisons between the qualities that Her Ladyship possessed and those of other women.

'If I lived for another hundred years I would not meet another woman to compare with Her Ladyship,' he once remarked.

There was another reason that convinced me that His Lordship would not marry a second time. He was very conscious of his ancestral line; a fresh marriage and the possibility of further children could have thrown it all into disarray and would have affected the titles and inheritances of Lady Patricia and Lady Pamela. Besides, he was now a grandfather many times over and his fits of loneliness would dissolve in the echo of children's feet whenever the family descended on Broadlands.

Lord Brabourne and Lady Patricia had quite a brood and while I failed to summon sufficient courage to tell his young Lordship to ease up, I did look him straight in the eye when the latest of the carrycots contained twins Nicholas and Timothy. We were running out of rooms. I think His Lordship, now the father of seven, got the message!

Lady Pamela and Mr Hicks also had three youngsters, naming their eldest daughter Edwina and their son Ashley after Lady Louis' family name Edwina Ashley. They called their second daughter India after the country so associated with His Lord and Ladyship.

There were new arrivals, too, from Buckingham Palace: Prince Andrew and Prince Edward, while our days were shortening!

In the summer of 1965, His Lordship announced his retirement from active duty and the Queen invested him with the Military Order of Merit. I really couldn't see Lord Louis retiring and, risking his wrath, I told him so.

'It's all hokum pokum,' I said.

'Yes, Charles, it is,' said His Lordship, 'but at least I will have more time to spend at Broadlands.'

Of course it was wishful thinking on His Lordship's part. Civilian life was ready to harness and exploit his expertise in all fields. In the not too distant future he was to serve as International President of the United World Colleges, a project aimed at promoting international understanding through education.

The Queen made him Governor of the Isle of Wight, and when the island gained county recognition, he was also made Lord Lieutenant.

The Government asked him to spearhead an inquiry into prison security. Any time left on his hands was consumed by the activities of the eighty world-wide organizations and associations to which he was affiliated either as patron or president.

His 'military' days weren't really over either. Within a month of his so-called retirement he was appointed Life Colonel Commandant of the Royal Marines, while continuing to occupy the rank of Colonel of the Life Guards.

Meanwhile at Broadlands His Lordship was very much involved with the local Territorial Army, having presented the unit with its colours. In 1967 the unit was to disband and Colonel Philip Powell suggested that His Lordship might consider allowing the farewell ball for 800, officers and men and their guests to be staged at Broadlands.

Lord Louis wrote back to Colonel Powell saying, 'It would be very nice to hold the ball at Broadlands, but I'm afraid I can't give you permission unless Charles Smith agrees.'

His Lordship showed me the letter at his desk and said, 'There you are, Charles. I am leaving the decision entirely to you because I know that you will have to bear the brunt of the organization and I don't want to land that on you without consulting you first.'

A ball at Broadlands on that scale was quite an operation, but with the help of the T.A. I managed to cope with it; Colonel Powell sent me a letter of congratulation.

Lord Louis liked being a host and some guests used to arrive by helicopter, landing their craft on the rear lawn! Industrialist Sebastian Ferranti always came by helicopter, and so did young Tommy Sopwith of the aviation family. And it was not uncommon to see either Prince Philip or Prince Charles step out of a helicopter, which they took delight in piloting to Broadlands!

There was always something happening. In neighbouring Southampton a new pub was named after His Lordship. He performed the opening ceremony, to which surviving members of the H.M.S. *Kelly* were also invited. Because His Lordship's car had a flat tyre, we travelled there in my Triumph Herald. One of his former Naval chums noted this and said, 'This isn't your car, Lord Louis?'

'No,' he replied, 'it's my butler's.' Then he laughed. 'I can afford to keep a butler, but I can't afford a car. Not as a pensioner!'

H.M.S. *Kelly* often figured in his thoughts. A local school submitted pictures of the destroyer drawn by the children for a special project and asked His Lordship to judge them. He was touched by the thought and sent a signed framed copy of an original master's painting of H.M.S. *Kelly* to the school.

The Life and Times of Lord Mountbatten

To Charles Smith
who entered my life
at about page 52
with best wishes for Xmas

Mountbatten of Burma

BROADLANDS.
ROMSEY.
HAMPSHIRE.
SO5 9ZD.

TELEPHONE
ROMSEY 3333.

24th June, 1970

My dear Charles,

I doubt whether any butler has been called upon to run such a stupendous weekend without bringing in a catering company to help him.

You planned everything brilliantly. However tired you must have been you were cheerful and kept up a wonderful show.

All my family were most impressed and asked me to express again to you their gratitude and appreciation.

I enclose a note which you may care to put on the notice board as it is addressed to the whole staff.

your ever

Mountbatten of Burma

Lord Louis' past was now to occupy his future, for he travelled back to Malta, Burma, India and the Far East to film a twelve-part television series called *The Life and Times of Lord Mountbatten*, which subsequently appeared as a book also.

Broadlands, too, was to ring with such memories when His Lordship celebrated his seventieth birthday on 25 June 1970. Prince Charles and other members of the Royal family, together with the monarchy of the European houses, were to spend a weekend of celebrations with us. Some thirty guests were accommodated in the house and local hotels took the overspill.

The fact that it was mid-summer helped greatly. The new swimming pool, which had been the birthday gift of Mrs Carola Rothschild of the famous Rothschild family, was ready in time, and in the Orangery a kitchenette and bar had been built. Red and white striped tents of an Eastern appearance, designed by David Hicks, lent a special atmosphere to the scene, while brightly coloured bucket chairs were hung from the branches of the nearby trees.

I enlisted the aid of Lady Brecknock's butler, Lady Sopwith's butler, and a local caterer, John Williams, to help with the preparation and service of the meals – the fare including salmon, trout, gammon, turkey, tongue, beef, lamb, duck, chicken, and veal, with all sorts of salads and fruit dishes, not to mention caviare and *pâté de foie*.

On the Monday morning, as the last of our guests departed, Lord Louis patted me on the shoulder and said, 'Charles, that was the best birthday party of my life. Only one person was missing. I wish she had been alive to see it.'

14

The Last Farewell

It had been a long and winding road. Now His Lordship, although eight years my senior, was to leave me flagging. His energy was boundless, he never seemed to tire. How much I envied his stamina!

Strenuous Naval affairs, matters of State, the complexities and problems of life in general, held no visible strain for him. Indeed, they served only to fuel his adrenalin. But for me, telling signs of stress and strain were to appear, and in early 1973 I suffered a nervous breakdown. Lord Louis insisted that I should take a long rest and sent me to Jersey to recuperate. Violet, of course, came with me and we stayed on the island for a fortnight.

It was incredible. Lord Louis rallied all his friends in Jersey to make us welcome and we were invited to the very beautiful home of Sir Billy Butlin. Sir Billy took us all over the house and when Violet mentioned she kept a budgerigar at home, the genial holiday-camp tycoon said, 'Then you had better come and look at mine!'

He showed us to an aviary in the grounds where he had a collection of 500!

When we returned home a letter was waiting for us from the Turks and Caicos Islands in the Bahamas. It was from Prince Charles, aboard H.M.S. *Minerva*, who had heard about my exhaustion.

The Prince, who had not long left Broadlands, wrote :

BROADLANDS,
ROMSEY,
HAMPSHIRE.
SO5 9ZD.

TELEPHONE
ROMSEY 3333.

7ᵗʰ March 1973

My dear Charles,

I send you very very best wishes for your 65ᵗʰ birthday and am glad to hear you are making a good recovery.

It is essential for you to really rest up and take care of yourself, please, as all the family are so very fond of you

Yours sincerely

Mountbatten of Burma

H.M.S. Minerva,   March 14th
    Turks + Caicos Islands   1973.

Dear Charles,

I was dreadfully sorry
to hear from His Lordship
that you had been so
unwell shortly after I
left Broadlands. I do hope
it was not my fault
and the accumulated result
of all the extra hard
work I have given you

of recent months?

I can't bear to think of you being unwell so whatever it is please get well soon. Broadlands won't be Broadlands without you and I can't think what Lord Mountbatten will do without you either. To say nothing of what I will do without you.

I think you will have to come out to this

glorious part of the world
and recuperate gently –
All this sunshine and
warm sea. I'm sure it
would do you good !

   Anyway I do hope Mrs.
Smith is looking after you
well and taking care of
every need and that you
have all you need. What-
ever happens make a rapid
recovery and have a really

good ~~luck~~ holiday + I
shall look forward to
seeing you = the autumn
again.

Yours sincerely

Charles.

'I do hope it was not my fault and the accumulated result of all the extra work I have given you of recent months? I can't bear to think of you being unwell so whatever it is please get well soon. Broadlands won't be Broadlands without you and I can't think what Lord Mountbatten will do without you either. To say nothing of what I will do without you.'

The letter, reproduced here in full, cheered me greatly and was a tonic to my recovery. When I went back to work, His Lordship was pleased to see me and said, 'From now on you must take things easier, Charles. We don't want you keeling over again. Whatever extra help you need, we will get it.'

I am sure I could have relied more on the rest of the staff, but I did not want to burden them with my work. Lord Louis demanded perfection; it was my responsibility to ensure these standards were maintained.

A butler's province is strictly a personal one, where trust, reliability and efficiency come uppermost in his duties. More and more I felt I was drifting; I was genuinely frightened of letting His Lordship down. It was time to call a halt. I was sixty-six. And now I had to tell Lord Louis.

'You retired when you were sixty-five, m'Lord,' I reminded Lord Louis, deciding that attack was the best form of defence.

'You're quite right,' said Lord Louis, 'but it only created more work for you, didn't it Charles?'

He smiled warmly. His Lordship knew I was tired and he also knew that I would never be able to leave Broadlands for good.

'When you've got a special function on, m'Lord, or if you need me at any time, you will only have to ring and I will come immediately,' I assured him.

'That is kind of you, Charles,' said Lord Louis, 'I know I can count on you.'

Lord Louis' grandson, Norton, was upset by my decision to retire and viewed it differently.

'I think you are being very disloyal, Charles,' he said, agitated to think that I might be letting his grandfather down.

'Disloyal? After fifty years, Mr Norton?' I said. 'I've given my life to Lord Louis and I'm still giving it now. I may be retiring but I'm not deserting the ship. I shall still be here whenever your grandfather needs me.'

Mr Norton bit his tongue and apologized.

'I'm sorry, Charles,' he said, 'I should not have doubted your loyalty. It is just hard for me to comprehend the thought of you leaving Lord Louis' service.'

I stayed on at Broadlands for another three months preparing the way for Mr George Daborn, my successor, and although it was a sad day when I officially retired, there were no farewell handshakes because it was generally believed that I would be back.

At first I kept well out of things, trying not to interfere in Mr Daborn's province. It was only fair that he should be given a free hand, without the thought of me lurking in the background.

I missed Broadlands through this period and not knowing what to do with myself I began to drink. I could not adapt to my new life in retirement. Lord Louis, on his frequent visits to the stable yard flat which he allowed us to continue to occupy, realized that I was heading for another breakdown and that I was trying to drink my way out of it.

He sent me to a psychiatrist, refusing to listen to my meanderings on the line that after fifty years 'there's no way I'm going to land up on a shrink's couch.'

His Lordship retaliated, 'Poppycock. Of course you're going to go.'

And go, reluctantly, I did!

In truth, the psychiatrist was more than understanding. His timely words effected a swift cure and the looming breakdown was averted. What was more, Violet could leave the gin bottle about the house without having to hide it!

Lord Louis signalled my recovery by asking me to assist at a special party being thrown at Broadlands for the start of the shooting season. Mr Daborn was pleased to see me and so were the old staff. Very soon I was a regular 'part-timer' among them and they made me feel very welcome.

Whatever my position, I knew that the special relationship I had forged with Lord Louis through the years would never be lost.

Even at this stage we could still find room to air our grievances.

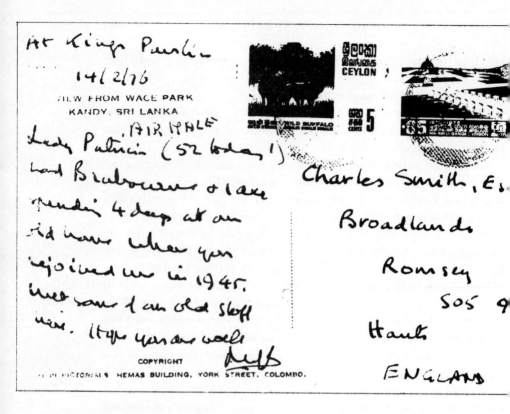

When Kelly, His Lordship's dog, was killed in a road accident, I must confess I was furious.

The dog had followed one of His Lordship's morning riding parties and was mown down when it ran across a main road. Maybe it was unjust of me, but I blamed Lord Louis.

'You should never have allowed the dog to have followed you, m'Lord,' I remonstrated. 'How could you hope to look after Kelly as well as the whole bloody riding party?'

His Lordship's feelings for Kelly were almost as deep as they had been for Pancho, and he felt upset at the dog's tragic end. My sharp words didn't really help matters but His Lordship must have dwelt on them because he came to see me with watery eyes, and putting his hand on my shoulder said, 'I'm sorry, Charles. Kelly should not have come out with us, but there is nothing more I can say now.'

Another of Lord Louis' Labradors, Juno, had nine puppies which

I helped raise through the first ten weeks and a present was made of one to Mrs Christina Ford, the wife of the American car magnate Henry Ford, who were regular visitors. Intending to compliment His Lordship, Mrs Ford named the pup 'Dickie', not realizing it was a bitch!

'Fancy doing that!' remarked Lord Louis.

Two years after my retirement, I was still living with Violet in the stable yard flat. There had been no rush for us to move. When we did finally leave the stable yard flat our new home was to be a sunny maisonette in the Edwina Mountbatten House only a stone's throw from Broadlands' main gates!

I helped His Lordship's archivist, Molly Travis, catalogue the huge volume of documents, letters, and photographs he had collected, and I also continued to be invited to the traditional staff Christmas parties at the house, when Lord Louis loved to be surrounded by his family, and especially his grandchildren, for the festivities.

None of us could have realized that Christmas 1978 was to be the last Yuletide that we would celebrate in Lord Louis' presence. As always it was a happy reunion of the family and Violet and I received presents from every member of the family, a gesture that meant a lot to us.

Spring came with a bustle, for in May 1979 His Lordship, with Prince Charles performing the official ceremony, was to open Broadlands to the public.

Violet scolded Lord Louis. 'It's not right, m'Lord. Why are you doing it?'

And I chipped in my word, as always. 'They'll ruin the house, m'Lord, all those people running through it.'

Lord Louis shook his head, understanding our fears.

'I've got to do it,' he said, 'I can't afford to keep Broadlands going otherwise.'

It wasn't His Lordship's intention to compete on the same commercial lines in the stately homes league as Lord Montagu of Beaulieu or the Duke of Bedford's Woburn Abbey.

'We will open the house as it is, without any gimmicks,' promised Lord Louis.

His Lordship kept closely to his word and the only point he conceded in the way of 'gimmicks' was to create a museum of the family archives, which he felt would be instructional and of genuine interest to the public.

Charts, maps and letters tracing his antecedents were put on display along with relics and souvenirs of his Lordship's own career through his war days with H.M.S. *Kelly* and as Supreme Allied Commander. Prize exhibits were the Japanese surrender swords, shown together with the pens used to sign the actual treaty. Into the museum also went his Viceroy of India robes, and an array of medals and trophies.

It was an inspiring collection and one I knew only too well! For that reason, I was pleased when I was asked to be one of the official guides to the house.

'No one knows the house, or our history as a family, better than you, Charles,' said Lord Louis.

It was a happy summer and masses of people descended on Broadlands, an impressive sight which provoked His Lordship to reflect, 'You know, Charles, we made the right decision. What matters to me most is how rewarding it is to share Broadlands with others.'

A fortnight before Lord Louis left for Ireland for his usual family holiday at Classiebawn Castle he called on me at the maisonette. Amanda, one of his grandchildren was with him, and Violet prepared some tea and scones.

With more time on my hands, I had started writing my book and I showed Lord Louis the first fifty-odd pages of the manuscript.

He was delighted and began reading it over tea.

'Charles,' he said, 'this is marvellous stuff. There are so many things you've mentioned that I'd almost forgotten.'

His Lordship chuckled. 'You know, Charles, I've still got that Panama hat . . . and do you remember that grey flannel suit of mine you gave away?'

He turned to Amanda and said, 'What do you think of a valet who would do a thing like that to you?'

Amanda was highly amused and was jumping up and down with excitement as she listened to our conversation.

As he put the manuscript down Lord Louis said, 'You've got to finish it, Charles. It will make a marvellous book.'

Our conversation turned to Ireland and his holiday plans. His daughter and son-in-law, Lord and Lady Brabourne, were going with him, and Lord Brabourne's mother, the Dowager Lady Brabourne, as well as the children.

'We're all looking forward to it, Charles,' he said, 'I hope the weather keeps fine. We will see you when we get back.'

Bidding farewell to Lord Louis at the door was to be the last time I saw him alive. I still held my manuscript in my hand, not contemplating that the last, fateful chapter loomed so near.

The I.R.A. struck without warning.

At the funeral service in Westminster, His Lordship's mare, Dolly, the horse he rode for the Trooping the Colour and other State ceremonies, was led in homage in the procession.

In Romsey Abbey, I kept vigil with three other elders of the staff before His Lordship's coffin was finally laid to rest. It was the saddest day of my life and one that still haunts me.

In the autumn we all had to put on a brave face and try to find the cheerfulness that Lord Louis spoke of. For his eldest grandson, Norton, was to marry Miss Penelope Eastwood, whose wedding had been arranged with the help of Lord Louis before the tragedy.

I think Romsey and the nation knew just how much strain might be placed on Norton and Penelope in their hour of happiness and all our thoughts were with them.

Try as we might we could not give way to a tinge of sadness – especially when Lord and Lady Brabourne, both badly hurt in the I.R.A. explosion, were pushed into the Abbey in wheelchairs. They had also lost Nicholas and the Dowager in the explosion, and Nicholas's twin brother, Timothy, suffered a temporary impairment in one eye caused by the blast.

I looked at the stone where Lord Louis was laid to rest and I cried a silent tear; what a cruel tragedy it had been.

But this was a wedding and it was a time for joy, and people of Romsey did their best to make it that way, especially with Her Majesty the Queen and Prince Philip present, and Prince Charles as Norton's best man.

With Violet I was invited to the reception at Broadlands. I saw many faces I knew from the past. Suddenly I found myself talking to Her Majesty, who asked me how I was getting on.

'Things aren't really the same without His Lordship, Your Majesty,' I replied.

Her Majesty said quietly, 'It can never be the same again for any of us, Charles.'

Nor can it be.

No man is a hero to his valet? What mockery Lord Louis made of that saying. In my eyes he will forever remain a hero.

Epilogue

If you can talk with crowds and keep your virtue,
*   Or walk with Kings – nor lose the common touch,*
If neither foes nor loving friends can hurt you,
*   If all men count with you, but none too much;*
If you can fill the unforgiving minute
*   With sixty seconds' worth of distance run,*
Yours is the Earth and everything that's in it,
*   And – which is more – you'll be a Man, my son!*

From *If–* by Rudyard Kipling

Index

abdication of Edward VIII, 53–4
Adsdean, 25; assembly of household
staff at, 34; bicycle polo at, 37–8;
golf at, 38
Alfonso, King of Spain, 29–30, 42, 94
Alice, Princess of Greece, 125–6, 129
Andrew, Prince, 153
Anne, Princess, 118
Attlee, Clement, 75, 106

Beg, Abdul, 87
Beg, Wally, 87
bicycle polo, 37–8
Birch, Arthur, 106
Bozo (bush baby), 40, 42, 43–4, 73
Brabourne, Lord, 104, 105, 119, 153;
marriage, 73–5; injured in I.R.A.
explosion, 169
Brabourne, Hon. Nicholas, 11, 153,
169
Brabourne, Hon. Norton, 105, 164–5,
169
Brabourne, Lady Patricia, *see* Mount-
batten, Lady Patricia
Brabourne, Hon. Timothy, 153, 169
Brecknock, Lady, 86
Brinz, Joe, 91, 92, 94
Britannia, Royal yacht, 141

Broadlands, 71–2; opened to public,
10, 167–8; domestic duties at,
90–101; dinner parties at, 94; security system at, 112; dry rot at, 131;
restoration, 131–2; family archives
museum, 168
Brook House, 21–7; reconstruction, 33
Buckingham Palace, 112–13
Butlin, Sir Billy, 158

Cartland, Barbara, 94
Ceylon, 64–5
Chaplin, Charlie, 40–1, 114
Chaplin, Oona, 114
Charles, Prince, 106, 154, 157; his
hamster, 118–19; confusion of name
with Smith's, 134–5; Lord M.'s
influence on him, 140–1; letter after
Charles Smith's breakdown,
158–64; opens Broadlands to
public, 167
Chester Street residence, 75
Churchill, (*later* Sir) Winston, 65, 111;
on Gandhi, 79; appoints Lord M.
First Sea Lord, 114
Classiebawn Castle, 11, 144, 168
Coward, Noël, 29, 61, 114; gala open-
ing of *Sail Away*, 145

Daborn, George, 165
Daring, H.M.S., 39
Darmstadt Palace, 56
Dawson, Montague, 145
Derby, Lady, 19–20
Derby, Lord, 19–20
Docker, Sir Bernard, 119
Docker, Lady, 119

Eastwood, Penelope, 169
Edward VIII, *see* Windsor, Duke of
Edward, Prince, 153
Edward, Prince of Wales, *see* Windsor, Duke of
Elizabeth II, 42–3, 72–3; marriage, 82–3; honeymoon at Broadlands, 84–6; Coronation, 110; visits Smiths' restored cottage, 116–17; at shoots at Broadlands, 117–18; at Broadlands, 136–7; presents Lord M. with Labrador dog, 137; at wedding of Hon. Norton Brabourne, 169–70
Ernest Louis, Grand Duke of Hesse, 56, 57

Fairbanks, Douglas, 40
Ferranti, Sebastian, 154
Ford, Christina, 167
Ford, Henry, 167
Fort Belvedere, 53

Gandhi, Mahatma, 79–80; assassination, 81–2
Geddes, Hon. Margaret, 57
George V, 51
George VI, 54–5, 73–5; on Lord M.'s appointment as Viceroy of India, 77; death, 108
George, Prince, *see* Kent, Duke of
Gloucester, Duke of, 111–12
golf at Adsdean, 38
Grant, Cary, 114
Gustav, King of Sweden, 113–14, 149

Hesse, Grand Duke Ernest Louis of, 56
Hesse, Prince Louis of, 57

Hesse, Princess Victoria of, 22
Hicks, David, 123, 157
hoax telephone calls, 26
Howes, Lieutenant Commander, 75

I.R.A. attack on Lord M.'s yacht, 10–11

Japanese surrender, 66–7

Kandy, Ceylon, 64–5
Kelly, H.M.S., 54, 101, 154; construction, 58; launching, 58; active service, 60; sunk, 60–1
Kelly (Labrador dog), 152, 166
Kensington Palace, 35–7, 104
Kent, Duke of (Prince George), 26–7, 35, 59; death in air crash, 60
Knowsley Hall, 19–20

Lee Lodge, 72
Lindbergh, Charles, 19
Louis, Prince of Hesse, 57
Louise, Queen of Sweden, 145, 149

Maclaine, Shirley, 114
Malta, 27–32, 38–40
Margaret, Princess, 42, 73
Marina, Princess of Greece and Denmark, 35
marriage, success of, 98
Mary, Queen, 33–4
Menon, Krishna, 88–9
Milford Haven, Dowager Marchioness of, 35, 104
Milford Haven, Marquess of, 57
Mountbatten of Burma, Earl: his funeral plans, 12–13; Senior Instructor at Portsmouth Signals School, 22; clothes, 25, 45–9; Fleet Wireless Officer, 27; in Malta, 27–32; promoted to commander, 31; polo, 38; second period in Malta, 38–40; adapts zip fastener for trousers, 45; sartorial aids, 45–6; mistaken for valet, 46–7; Panama hat, 49–50; with Edward VIII before abdication, 53–4; and Duke of Windsor,

Mountbatten of Burma, Earl—*cont.* 54; command of H.M.S. *Kelly*, 58, 60–1; in Ceylon, 64–5; decoration box, 64–5; in Singapore, 65–9; at Broadlands, 72
appointed Viceroy of India, 75; leaves for India, 77; 'swearing-in' ceremony, 77–9; and Gandhi, 79–80, 81–2; returns to England, 86; suite at Broadlands, 90; life at Broadlands, 91–101; married life, 98–9; character, 98, 99–100; promoted Vice-Admiral, 106; Commander-in-Chief, Mediterranean, 106–7; appointed Fourth Sea Lord, 108; death of his mother, 108; appointed personal A.D.C. to Queen, 112; appointed First Sea Lord, 115
after Lady Mountbatten's death, 129, 131; gift of Labrador dog from Queen, 137; shoots lady in foxtail wrap, 140; influence on Prince Charles, 140–1; concern for Smiths' well being, 145; disinclination to remarry, 152–3; retirement from active service, 153; invested with Military Order of Merit, 153; International President of United World Colleges, 153; Governor of Isle of Wight, 153; Life Colonel Commandant of Royal Marines, 154; and Territorial Army, 154; films television series on his life and times, 157; seventieth birthday, 157; last holiday at Classiebawn Castle, 168–9; funeral, 169

Mountbatten, Lady Edwina: family background, 22; clothes, 24–5, 80; seaplane flight to Malta, 38–9; conducts 'Operation Mercy', 67; inherits Broadlands, 71; tiara designed by Lord M., 76; and marriage of Princess Elizabeth, 84; suite at Broadlands, 90; character, 98–9; married life, 98–9; loss of tiara, 112–13; flower arranging, 121; concern with domestic matters, 122;

Charles sends for vet, 122–3; leaves on Far East tour, 123; death in Borneo, 124–5

Mountbatten, Lady Pamela, 27, 42, 145; first birthday, 23–4; in Malta, 30; 'coming out' ball, 114; marriage, 123

Mountbatten, Lady Patricia, 24, 27, 42, 145; in Malta, 30; marriage, 73–5; birth of first child, 104–6; her children, 119, 153

Mount Batten, R.A.F., 59

Mount Temple, Lord, 57, 71

Nehru, Pandit, 80, 87; yoga exercises, 87–8

Norway, King of, 97

O'Grady, Paddy, 144

Pakistan, 79

Pancho (Labrador dog), 137, 150–2

Patel, Sardar, 80

Perkins, Detective Inspector, 85

pets, Mountbattens': Bozo the bush baby, 40, 42, 43–4, 73; dogs, 137, 150–2; Rastas the honey bear, 30–1; Sabi the lion cub, 40, 41–2

Philip, Prince, 154, 169; at Lee Lodge, 7; at Kensington Palace, 35–7; marriage, 82–3; honeymoon at Broadlands, 84–6; visit to Smiths' restored cottage, 116; attends Lady M.'s funeral, 125

Pickford, Mary, 40

polo, bicycle, 37–8

Portland, Duchess of, 17, 18–19

Portland, Duke of, 17

Powell, Colonel Philip, 154

Rainier, Prince, 119

Randall, Frank, 83, 84, 115

Rastas (honey bear), 30–1

Romsey Abbey, 12, 13

Rothschild, Carola, 157

Rutherford, Arthur, 39

Sabi (lion cub), 40, 41–2

Sargent, Sir Malcolm, 114
shooting parties at Broadlands, 117–18
Simpson, Wallis, see Windsor, Duchess of
Sinatra, Frank, 114
Singapore, 65–9
Slim, General Sir William, 65
Smith, Charles: family background, 15–16; childhood, 16–17; work in coal mine, 17; at Welbeck Abbey, 17–19; at Knowsley Hall, 19–20; arrival at Brook House, 25–6; in Malta, 27–32; at Kensington Palace, 35–7; second period in Malta, 38–40; Panama hat, 49–50; meets Mrs Simpson, 52; enlists in R.A.F., 59; transferred to India, 61; arrested for writing to Lord M., 61–2; in Ceylon, 64–5; in Singapore, 65–9; cited in divorce case, 68; returns to England, 69; marriage, 69; temporary administrative post after war, 72
    Lord M.'s appointment as Viceroy of India, 75–6; the flight to India, 77; preparing Lord M.'s Viceregal robes, 78–9; Gandhi's visit to Government House, 78–9; Gandhi's assassination, 81–2
    arranges honeymoon for Princess Elizabeth and Prince Philip, 84–6; with Lady Brecknock at Liphook, 86; domestic duties at Broadlands, 90–101; with Lady Patricia Brabourne before birth of her first child, 104–5; Coronation preparations, 110–11; stays at Buckingham Palace, 112–13; promoted to butler, 115; restores dilapidated cottage, 116; sends vet when Lady M. ill, 122–3; confusion of name with Prince Charles', 134–5; telephone voice mistaken for Lord M.'s, 135–6; on Royal yacht Britannia, 141; at Buckingham Palace garden party, 141–4; at Queen's silver wedding anniversary service, 144; holiday at Classiebawn Castle, 144; arranges Territorial Army ball at Broadlands, 154; nervous breakdown, 158–64; retirement, 164–5; psychiatric help, 165
Smith, Shirley, 69–70, 112
Smith, Violet, 68, 106, 108, 113–14
Sopwith, Tommy, 154
Spencer, Mr (Lord M.'s butler), 21–3
Sweden, King Gustaf of, 113–14, 149

Taylor, Elizabeth, 114
Territorial Army, 154
This Is Your Life, Lord M. subject of, 9–10
Travis, Mollie, 14, 167
Truman, President, 65

United World Colleges, 153

Valletta, 27, 38–9
Victoria, Queen, 22
Victoria, Princess of Hesse, 22
Victoria and Albert (Royal yacht), 55

Ward, Elizabeth, 112–13
Wavell, Lord, 75
Webb, Commander, 75
Welbeck Abbey, 17–19
Wernher, Lady Anastasia 'Zia', 133
Wernher, Sir Harold, 133
Wight, Isle of, 153
Wilding, Michael, 114
Windsor, Duchess of, 52–3, 97, 152
Windsor, Duke of, 26, 51, 53–4, 97
Wishart, H.M.S., 39
Women's Lib, 98–9

York MW102 (Lord M.'s aircraft), 65–6, 76–7

Zeppelin raids, 16
zip fasteners, 44